SKINNY
SNACKS

KAREN PROTHEROE

NEW
HOLLAND

CONTENTS

FOREWORD

We all take a slightly Jekyll and Hyde approach to food and eating.

The controlled, responsible self eats a balanced, high-fibre breakfast, makes sure to get a modest portion of protein, some complex carbohydrates and plenty of crunchy salads and vegetables at the other meals, disdains the crackling on the pork and the cream on the dessert, crunches an apple when the munchies hit, and practises moderation around coffee, wine and anything else that becomes toxic in quantity.

But there's the other self. The one that's too rushed for breakfast, hits a takeaway when tummy rumbles kick in, settles the late afternoon slump with a chocolate, goes into the evening meal feeling starved, and, not to put too fine a point on it, is both malnourished and semi-toxic most of the time.

That's why this book is such a godsend. Karen Protheroe is all too familiar with nutritional horror stories. Her conclusion: it's futile to pretend we do the three-square-meals thing. We're a society of snackers. The intelligent response is to harness that reality – to understand what lies behind, and constructively engage with, our snacking habit, and enlist it for our bodies' health.

Which fits in nicely, of course, with our current conviction that five or six small meals a day is healthier than three bigger ones (and certainly a lot healthier than the two rounds of junk food and a pig-out that characterises so many peoples' 'meal planning'). So *Skinny Snacks* sets out to blur our conceptual boundaries between a meal (big, a mission to prepare) and a snack (small, quick, convenient), and outline an eating philosophy based on our snacking reality. Find out about how to enlist snacks to boost your metabolism, what the glycaemic index is all about, tricks you can play on yourself when you feel a destructive snack attack coming on, a fabulous line up of quick-fix ideas, tricks for how to cope in situations ranging from restaurants to rugby games, and a line-up of plans for every lifestyle. If you want to lose or gain weight, are male or female, active or inactive; if you need to build muscle or increase energy, if you're an emotional eater, a picky eater or going through trauma (such as giving up smoking) – this book addresses your specific issues. It's interesting, practical, substantial yet accessible. A bit like a snack, really.

Congratulations on buying it, and keep it close. I know I will.

HEATHER PARKER
Editor, **Shape** magazine

If my successful clients return to consult with me because they have regained a bit of weight, six months, one year or even longer after stopping our consultations, it is usually not because they have been eating high-fat foods or consuming hidden fats; they still cook without oil, only use fat-free dairy products, and avoid margarine and butter. The most common reason for their return is that they have slipped back into the habit of skipping meals and snacks and are only eating one or two large meals a day instead of five or six meals or snacks. This results in overeating, bingeing and, often, unhealthy, hastily chosen food.

The terms 'meals' and 'snacks' are used throughout the book, but they are deemed to be the same in both definition and content.

INTRODUCTION

Snacks play several roles in our lives and mean different things to different people. What a snack is to one person, is a meal to another. Snacks can be sweet or savoury, hot or cold, liquid or solid. Snacks should, generally speaking, be small, require little or no preparation and should be fairly easy to handle. Snacks can be a form of comfort food and can take you back to your childhood when you fell and scraped your knee and your mother mopped up your tears with a little love and usually something sweet. Warm snacks are favourites in winter when it is raining or freezing cold outside and you are warm and snug inside. Snacks can be a form of reward for completing a task or getting through the day, and can often form part of rituals; for example, if meeting a friend for a chat over a cup of coffee, a snack such as a biscuit or piece of cake seems to be a vital component of that meeting. The same applies to meeting someone for a drink – peanuts or crisps are a must; or eating popcorn and chocolate at the movies, and so on.

Snacks are becoming more and more important in the modern-day diet due to their transient, convenient, no-fuss guise. Most of us don't have time to eat a meal, let alone prepare one during the day, so we rely on so-called 'snack food' to replace these meals.

SNACKS
IN GENERAL

As a result, we generally eat one large (often very large!) meal in the evening and rely on a number of infrequent snacks during the day which are usually chosen for their handiness or availability rather than for their nutritional value.

You will be amazed to find that by eating more snacks during the day, your evening meal will become smaller without even trying to make it so.

This book comprises lists of snacks for everyone who is trying to manage their weight, be healthy or even to treat specific health problems such as constipation or high cholesterol. Most of the snacks listed are low in cholesterol and animal fats. The ideal Calorie content of a snack is anything up to 300 Calories, but this is not fixed. The ideal number of snacks is six snacks a day, eaten every 2–3 hours from when you first wake up.

I use the terms 'meals' and 'snacks' – I don't differentiate between the two and consider them interchangeable in both definition and content.

The aim of this book is to show you how you can lose weight effortlessly and permanently by eating more often. You will at the same time improve your health and energy levels. Even if your goal is weight maintenance or weight gain, snacking will help you achieve this goal.

A SURVEY OF THE
SNACKING HABITS OF MY CLIENTS

**I asked 44 of my clients (36 female, 8 male)
five questions about their snacking habits. Most
of them had been consulting me or one of my
colleagues for a while and therefore knew the
difference between healthy and fattening food,
and healthy and low-fat food.**

ARE YOU A SWEET OR SAVOURY SNACKER?

**There seems to be a trend for women to have more of a sweet
tooth while men prefer savoury snacks.** It was quite surprising for
me, however, to find that my female clients were almost split
down the middle, with half preferring sweet and the other half
preferring savoury. About 30% of both sexes had both sweet and
savoury cravings at different times of the day, and this could
change seasonally. I have noticed that many people prefer sweet
things in winter and savoury snacks in summer. (Perhaps the loss
of salt caused by sweating during summer makes us crave salty
foods.) Some women also find that their craving for sweet or
savoury foods depends on where they are in their menstrual cycle.

WHEN IS YOUR FAVOURITE TIME OF THE DAY
TO SNACK?

**The most popular time of the day to snack, by a large margin, is
late afternoon or early evening when people get home from work
and feel the urge to snack before dinner.** This is usually because
most of us don't eat enough or often enough during the day when
we are busy and running around. Also, coming home from work
is a transient time and may be quite stressful or stress-releasing,
depending on your situation. Many women find it quite
difficult to go from career woman to wife, mother or
cook. Late evening, after dinner, was the next
favourite time to snack.

WHERE DO YOU MOST OFTEN GET THE URGE TO SNACK?

In front of the television is the most common place where snacking urges occur. Perhaps, apart from tempting food ads, television snacking could be a habit or ritual (like watching movies and eating popcorn). Also, when you collapse in front of the television at the end of a hard day, it may be the first time that you relax and may feel the urge to reward or comfort yourself.

Other common places for snacking are in the kitchen and at work. The kitchen is an obvious temptation spot as most snacks are kept here, and working with food without snacking is almost impossible when you are hungry. Snacking at work can be linked to social interaction (birthday cakes, functions, etc.) or to work stress or boredom. Also, if you don't make a plan to eat enough at work (either by taking in your own food or buying food at work), then snacking will be tempting when the snack cart rolls past your desk. The car is another fairly common spot for snacking – a symptom, it would appear, of our hectic, rushed lives.

Some snackers said that any time or place is good for snacking.

WHAT IS YOUR FAVOURITE UNHEALTHY SNACK?

Chips (crisps) rated as the most popular unhealthy snack, with chocolate coming a very close second. Pies, cake and cheese also received votes. Not so unhealthy, but rather high calorie snacks included nuts and muffins.

WHAT IS YOUR FAVOURITE HEALTHY, LOW-FAT SNACK?

Wine gums, jelly babies and marshmallows were voted as the healthy alternative to something sweet. All these sweets are fat free, but they contain sugar and must be eaten in moderation if weight is an issue. Other popular sweet snacks included fruit, yoghurt and malted milk powder with skimmed milk.

The most popular healthy alternative for those wanting a savoury snack, were crackers with either low-fat cheese or yeast extract (Marmite). Low-fat soups, crudités with a low-fat yoghurt dip, pretzels and popcorn were also fairly popular.

EATING SMALL, FREQUENT SNACKS
OR MEALS WILL HELP TO STABILIZE YOUR
BLOOD SUGARS

Blood sugars help to control your mood, your energy levels, your appetite and cravings and your metabolism and fat storage.

IDEAL BLOOD SUGARS
= constant mood

= constant energy levels

= controllable appetite without cravings

= maintenance of metabolism

= minimal fat storage

FLUCTUATING BLOOD SUGARS
= fluctuating mood – one minute overly excited and the next minute depressed or grumpy

= fluctuating energy levels – hyperactivity followed by sluggishness

= cravings, usually for something sweet

= more fat storage in the long term and body becomes more energy efficient, i.e. it uses less energy to function

WHAT CAUSES FLUCTUATING BLOOD SUGARS?
- **Skipping meals and snacks**, particularly breakfast, and then overeating when you do eat
- **Not eating enough carbohydrate**, for example, when on low-carbohydrate diets which are currently quite popular
- **Eating foods that are quickly absorbed**, such as refined (usually sugary and low-fibre) foods
- **Expending more energy than you are taking in**, for example, exercising for a long time on an empty stomach
- **Medical conditions** such as diabetes
- **Insufficient sleep**
- **Alcohol**

EATING SMALL, FREQUENT SNACKS WILL ENSURE THAT YOU DON'T NEED TO RELY ON **WILLPOWER**

- **Willpower is here today, gone tomorrow**; you can't rely on it. Any diet that requires you to rely on willpower and to say no to certain foods or to just stick to the diet will eventually fail.

- **Don't let yourself get hungry** – hungry people make unhealthy choices and eat too much, too quickly, whereas not-so-hungry people make healthier choices and are able to stop eating before they are over-full.

- **Not-so-hungry people are able to TASTE the wrong foods**; hungry people **FILL UP** on the wrong foods.

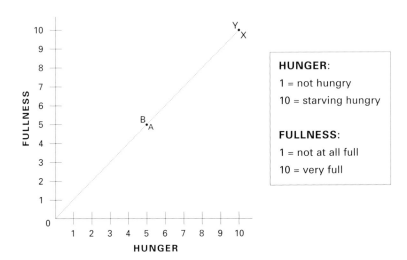

HUNGER:
1 = not hungry
10 = starving hungry

FULLNESS:
1 = not at all full
10 = very full

Diagram: If you eat when you are starving hungry (X), you will only stop eating when you are very full (Y). If you eat when you are only slightly peckish (A), you will be able to stop eating when you are comfortably full (B).

- **Make sure your hunger and fullness levels match up.** If you still overeat (Y) even when you aren't hungry (A), you may be eating for reasons other than physical hunger, such as emotional eating (see pages 74–76).

EATING SMALL, FREQUENT HIGH-CARBOHYDRATE SNACKS WILL HELP TO OPTIMIZE YOUR **METABOLISM**

We all know that people with 'slow metabolisms' seem to struggle with their weight, whereas those with high or 'fast metabolisms' are able to manage their weight more easily.

WHAT IS METABOLISM ALL ABOUT?

- **Your metabolism is basically your internal fire** that works like the fire in a steam train and drives all the processes in your body, from digesting your food to making your muscles contract and relax when exercising or at rest.

- **The fuel that feeds the fire is food**, preferably carbohydrates as this is the easiest fuel for the body to burn. Fatty food is like wet wood – it takes longer to burn.

- **If you don't continually put wood or coal on the fire it will eventually die down to coals** and any wood that is then thrown onto the fire will smoke and smoulder. When this happens in the body, the body struggles to burn any excess fuel (food) that is consumed.

- **It is also not sufficient to only put wood on the fire once a day;** it is necessary to keep the fire roaring so that no matter what gets thrown into it, the body will burn it up.

- **There are no scientifically proven foods, vitamins, minerals or other supplements that can increase your metabolism.** Grapefruit, chromium picolinate, kelp or even ginseng have not conclusively been shown to increase metabolism.

11

CAUSES OF A SLOW METABOLISM

- Starvation and fad diets
- Years of dieting and weight cycling
- Medical conditions (usually hormone based), such as thyroid problems
- Inactivity, which results in low muscle mass
- Ageing causes a natural decline in metabolism
- Genetics can also play a role

TO INCREASE YOUR METABOLISM

- Eat every 3–4 hours
- Eat 5–6 meals a day
- Eat carbohydrates at every meal or snack
- Eat complex carbohydrates, such as fruit or wholemeal products
- Drink plenty of water
- Eat small amounts of low-fat protein and unsaturated fats with your meals
- Eat breakfast every day – if you skip breakfast you won't get hungry until much later in the day because your metabolism won't start working until then
- Weight loss, an increased appetite and increased energy levels are common signs of an increased metabolism

'Your metabolism is basically your internal fire that works like the fire in a steam train and drives all the processes in your body.'

12

WHY YOU SHOULD EAT **LOW-FAT, HIGH-CARBOHYDRATE** SNACKS
TO LOSE WEIGHT

- **Satiety during the meal is dependent on your carbohydrate and protein intake, which means that you won't feel satisfied with that meal until you have eaten sufficient carbohydrates and protein.** Therefore, if you eat a meal that is high in fat with little carbohydrates and/or protein, you will tend to overeat and thereby take in too much fat.

- **Recent studies have shown that if you overeat on carbohydrates, your body will respond by increasing the rate at which it burns up carbohydrates.** However the same does not apply to fat. If you overeat on fats, the body is not capable of increasing its fat burning and this will result in increased fat storage and possible weight gain.

- **It is very difficult for the body to store excessive carbohydrates as fat stores,** whereas the body is very capable of storing excessive dietary fat as body fat.

- There are some new scientific theories being tested that show that **some people may be better fat burners** (they are less likely to gain weight if eating a high-fat diet), while **others are better carbohydrate burners** (they will maintain their weight as long as they stick to low-fat, high-carbohydrate diets). How these differences are determined or predicted is still being questioned, as well as how it will affect weight management.

- **Fat should not be totally removed from the diet** as it has many important functions in the body, such as providing important vitamins and essential fatty acids, protecting the organs and nerves, insulation and storage of energy. **Fat is valued for adding palatability to food and for producing a feeling of fullness after eating.** If you eat a meal that is low in fat or even fat free, it is normal for you to feel hungry again much sooner than if you eat a meal high in fat.

You get two basic types of fat, good unsaturated fat and poor saturated fat. However, because so many fats are hidden in our regular, everyday diet and are not always avoidable, we should make an effort to cut out the fat whenever it is in our power to do so. The hidden fat is usually of the poor saturated kind. Try to cut out the visible and hidden fats in your diet wherever possible and, when consciously adding fat to your diet, make sure it is of the unsaturated kind (see below).

GOOD UNSATURATED FATS
(healthy but still fattening –
includes most vegetable fats, except coconut)

1 SERVING

= 1 tsp (5 ml) soft margarine (sunflower or linseed)
= 2 tsp (10 ml) low-fat spread
= 1 tsp (5 ml) vegetable oil (sunflower, olive, rapeseed)
= 2 tsp (10 ml) peanut butter
= 2 walnuts or 4 almonds
= 1 Tbsp (15 ml) sunflower seeds
= ¼ avocado
= 6 olives

POOR SATURATED FATS
(unhealthy and fattening –
includes most animal fats and coconut fat)

1 SERVING

= 1 tsp (5 ml) butter or block margarines
= 1½ tsp (7.5 ml) medium-fat spread
= 1 tsp (5 ml) mayonnaise
= 2 tsp (10 ml) reduced-calorie salad cream
= 1 Tbsp (15 ml) single cream

1 G OF FAT PROVIDES 9 CALORIES (38 KJ) OF ENERGY

14

CARBOHYDRATE GROUP

1 SERVING   1 SERVING   1 SERVING   1 SERVING   1 SERVING

BREADS AND ROLLS
= 1 slice of bread (30 g) cut 1 cm thick
= ½ roll, bagel or pita

CRISPBREADS
= 2–4, depending on size

CEREALS
= ½ cup (125 ml) cooked porridge
= ¾ cup (180 ml) flake cereal
= 1 wheat cereal biscuit
= 1 cup (250 ml) puffed, unsweetened cereal
= ⅓ cup (80 ml) low-fat muesli

RICE AND PASTA
= ½ cup (125 ml) cooked rice, pasta or couscous

STARCHY VEGETABLES
= 1 medium potato
= 1 cup (250 ml) beetroot, squash, carrots,
  peas or pumpkin

LEGUMES
= ½ cup (125 ml) dried beans, peas, lentils – cooked

ALCOHOL
= 1 glass (125 ml) dry white or red wine
= 1 tot (25 ml) spirits
= ½ can (170 ml) beer or cider

**1 G OF CARBOHYDRATE PROVIDES
4 CALORIES (17 KJ) OF ENERGY**

LABELLING LEGISLATION

Many developed countries use international standards when it comes to food labelling. These govern the meaning of terms that are used on packaging, such as low fat, fat free and reduced fat, and specify when they can be used. Other terms that may be controlled are cholesterol free, no added sugar, sugar free and high fibre.

The use of descriptive names are defined: for example, a strawberry yogurt must contain a certain percentage of strawberries whereas a strawberry flavoured yogurt will only contain strawberry flavouring. There are also rules aimed at ensuring that no inaccurate or misleading claims or descriptions are used.

CHOOSING SNACKS WITH A LOW
GLYCAEMIC INDEX (GI) WILL HELP
TO STABILIZE YOUR BLOOD SUGARS AND
KEEP YOU FULL

WHAT IS THE GI?

- **All food and meals cause different responses to blood sugar levels**. Low GI foods release their sugar from that food, slowly and steadily over a prolonged period, into the bloodstream and prevent over-stimulation of the pancreas, which in turn reduces the production of insulin. This can be beneficial not only for the diabetic, but also for people wanting to lose weight. Insulin, needed to pull glucose into the muscle for energy, is what we call an anabolic or building hormone, and too much insulin in the bloodstream can cause fat storage. Therefore, eating slow-release food will minimize the negative effects of insulin.

- **Because low GI foods are absorbed slowly, they keep you fuller for longer**, which is great for those trying to control their appetites.

- **For those who suffer from low blood sugars, low GI foods will help maintain their blood sugar levels.** Consuming high GI foods can result in an immediate but short-lived increase in blood sugar levels, followed by a rapid drop.

- **Low GI foods tend to be high fibre foods.**

INTERESTING INFORMATION

Fibre fills you up (which means you will eat less) not only because it takes longer to chew but also because it absorbs water and swells. Fibre has a low GI as it takes a long time to break down and be absorbed. Insoluble fibre (roughage) can aid weight loss as it passes through the body without being absorbed, and therefore consists of empty Calories. Examples are edible fruit and vegetable peels, bran or wholemeal grains.

- **Adding small amounts of low-fat protein or unsaturated fats to your snack can also help to make you feel fuller for longer** as it lowers the GI of that snack.

- **The Glycaemic Index is also used for sports nutrition**, where high GI foods are used as a source of quick energy during and immediately after short and endurance exercise.

- **An interesting new use for low GI foods is in the prevention of heart disease.** Research has shown that lowering the GI of a diet can help improve good (HDL) cholesterol levels.

- **Many factors affect the GI of foods.** For example, cooking and cooling certain foods lowers their GI; cold potato salad (with reduced-calorie mayonnaise and yoghurt of course) has a lower GI than baked or boiled potatoes. Foods high in fibre, fat and protein tend to have a lower GI as they slow down the rate of digestion. Processed foods have a higher GI.

INTERESTING INFORMATION

To help the public make informed choices when buying foods many supermarket chains stamp foods with logos to indicate which are low in fat, and sometimes those that are low in cholesterol, or that are suitable for vegetarians, such as cheeses made using vegetarian rennet. So keep an eye on supermarket shelves for these products.

- **The main disadvantage of the marketing of GI foods, as with any other health foods, is that the public becomes obsessed.** Although low GI foods are of benefit in some circumstances, it doesn't mean that all foods marked with the low GI logo are healthy. Potato crisps, for example, have a low GI, but are still full of fat!

EXAMPLES OF HIGH AND LOW GI FOODS

LOWER GI FOODS	HIGHER GI FOODS
low-fat and fat-free dairy	sports drinks
seeded, heavy breads such as seedloaf or pumpernickel	white or brown bread or rolls, rice cakes, crispbreads
dried, cooked beans and lentils, boiled pasta	instant pasta
cooked, cooled potato (e.g. potato salad) or sweet potato	baked or mashed potato
citrus and deciduous fruit	dried fruit rolls, watermelon, tropical fruit
bran cereals, raw muesli, oats, oat bran	wheat cereal biscuits, puffed cereals, shredded wheat
basmati rice, soya	white or brown rice

GUIDELINES TO USING THE GI

- Eat soya and legumes as often as possible.
- When baking, substitute one-third to half of the flour with oat bran and continue with the recipe as usual.
- Choose biscuits/crackers made with oats, oat bran and soya.
- Choose high-fibre cereals or those containing soya.
- Stick to the portion sizes that you are allowed, and spread your carbohydrates into 5–6 meals or snacks throughout the day.
- If you eat a high GI food, try to combine it with a low GI food, e.g. a baked potato with baked beans.
- Learn to distinguish between low-fat, low GI and high-fat, low GI foods, and avoid the latter.
- Don't just rate food according to its GI; a varied diet is important.
- The recommendation for diabetics is to try and eat two low GI meals a day, and to keep all snacks between meals low GI.

WHY 'TOO MUCH' SKINNY SNACKING CAN SLOW DOWN **WEIGHT LOSS**

Too much of a good thing is nearly as bad for weight loss as too much of a bad thing. A common realization with many of my clients whose weight loss has slowed down is that, although they are successfully avoiding the high-fat foods, they are eating **too much** of the healthier foods. This is not usually a bad thing for weight maintenance or general health (especially if you are fairly active), but it will slow down your weight loss if you are trying to shed a few kilograms. Remember that it is the total Calories as well as the fat intake that need to be reduced in order to lose weight.

IF YOU ARE EATING TOO MUCH FRUIT AND CARBOHYDRATES
These foods are the preferred source of energy for the body. If you eat too much of them, however, your body will use up the excess that you consume and won't need to access its fat stores.

IF YOU ARE TAKING IN TOO MUCH PROTEIN
Too much protein, even the lower-fat protein such as white meat, ostrich or fish, means you still take in too much fat. A skinless chicken breast, which is grilled or poached, has 7 g of fat (this fat is invisible, but it is there) and a boiled egg has 5 g of fat. These fats are not only fattening, but can also have negative effects on blood cholesterol. Excessive amounts of protein can also place strain on your kidneys, which could be harmful in the long run.

FOODS OFTEN EATEN IN EXCESS

- 1 cup (250 ml) of skimmed **milk** adds 90 Calories (378 kJ)
- 1 slice of wholemeal **bread** adds 80 Calories (336 kJ)
- 1 **fruit** and extra glass of fruit juice adds 180 Calories (756 kJ)
- 1 Tbsp (15 ml) of reduced-calorie **salad dressing** adds 60 Calories (252 kJ)
- 1 skinless **chicken** breast adds 200 Calories (840 kJ)
- 1 glass (120 ml) of red **wine** adds 125 Calories (525 kJ)
- 1 cup (250 ml) of **pasta** adds 210 Calories (882 kJ)
- 1 quarter of an **avocado** adds 110 Calories (462 kJ)

= **Total added 1055 Calories (4431 kJ)**

To put this in perspective, an average inactive woman who wants to lose weight should not take in more than 1200–1500 Calories (5040–6300 kJ) a day.

If you are following an energy-restricted eating plan (which you need to do if you want to lose weight), then you can see how easy it is to take in too much energy even though most of the above foods are either low in fat or completely fat-free. Day after day, this can spell the difference between dropping weight (slowly as recommended) and not. Remember that to lose half a kilogram a week, you need to have a weekly deficit in total energy of 3500 Calories (14700 kJ), which works out at 500 Calories (2100 kJ) a day. (This figure will vary between individuals.) Exercise will help to increase this deficit.

TIPS FOR CONTROLLING PORTION SIZES

- **Work out how many portions of carbohydrate, protein, fat, fruit and dairy you need each day.** Either use my guidelines (see pages 63–65) or, even better, see a dietician for a personalized assessment.

- **Keep a brief record or diary for a few days of everything that you eat.** At the end of each day, calculate how many portions you have had too much or too little of from each of the food groups so that you will be aware of where you are going wrong.

- **Plan ahead for tomorrow** – work out briefly in your mind how you will reach your quota. Planning ahead means that you will be better organized as well as being less vulnerable to chance and temptation.

- **Every now and then, remember to recheck your portion sizes.** Use a measuring cup to measure out a cup of cooked pasta or cereal. It is amazing how, over time, the estimated portions get larger, not smaller.

- **Try to only purchase and prepare exactly how much you need for your meal;** having leftovers lying around is only going to tempt you. As soon as you have finished dishing up your meal, store the leftovers in a suitable container and place in the freezer or pack it into a lunchbox for the next day. If the leftovers are not of the kind that can be eaten the next day, throw them away – you are not the dustbin.

- **Remember not to skip a meal or snack** as you will be so hungry at the next meal that your allowed portion will not satisfy you.

- **If you are still hungry after eating your allowed portion, wait 15 minutes before making something else to eat.** Eat slowly and remember it is carbohydrate- and protein-rich foods that will fill you up at that meal.

- **Fill up on free vegetables** (see page 55). Have a free-vegetable soup or salad as a starter so that your main meal satisfies you.

- **When others dish up for you, they often dish up too much.** Tell yourself that you don't need to clean your plate (you may still remember your parents saying 'clean your plate and you may have dessert'); leave food on your plate – it is a liberating feeling.

- **Remind yourself that you will eat another meal in 2–3 hours** and therefore do not need to stockpile.

WHERE YOU SNACK CAN PLAY A ROLE IN WEIGHT LOSS

SOME TYPICAL PLACES WHERE UNHEALTHY SNACKING OCCURS
- **Standing** – snacks eaten standing in front of the fridge or stove are like broken biscuits – they don't count
- In the **kitchen**
- In the **car**
- In front of the **television or computer**
- At **work**
- In the queue at the **supermarket**
- At **restaurants** and coffee shops
- **Cocktail or drinks parties** where snacks are freely available
- In **bars**

TIPS TO CONTROL UNHEALTHY SNACKING

Setting rules makes it easier to control bad eating habits.

- **Never go shopping or start cooking when you are starving hungry** – always eat something first.

- **Never eat in the kitchen, in the car, at your desk or in front of the television.** Eat your meal or snack in the dining room, canteen, outside or in a place where you can sit in front of your food and focus all your attention on the nourishing and nurturing properties of that food.

- **Never eat standing up.**

- **Only eat using cutlery and crockery** – this will slow you down.

- **Once you have made your meal, pack all the ingredients away** before you eat so that it is a hassle to prepare another helping.

- **Once you have identified your area of weakness, it is easy to make the above rules and stick to them;** you will think twice before taking a teaspoon of mousse from the refrigerator, putting it on a plate and going to sit at the dining room table to eat it.

- **Be aware that times of transition, such as getting home from work, are often binge susceptible times,** so plan activities to distract or relax you to make the transition easier, such as going for a walk or going to the gym.

- **Make snack times an appointment** – put the times in your diary. Several of my clients find that they get caught up in work and forget to eat, so they set their cellular phones or desk organizers to beep at them every three hours to remind them.

- **Food has a nurturing as well as nourishing role to play.** We tend to nurture others by nourishing them, so do the same to yourself – hurriedly shoving lunch down your throat in the car is not nurturing and you won't feel satisfied, which can too easily result in overeating or looking for unhealthy foods to comfort you.

- **Pretend your home is a health hydro.** At home, eat only those foods that will enhance your health. Weight, health and energy maintenance is eating only healthy foods at home and relaxing when you eat out. If you hardly ever eat out, then eat only healthy foods during the week and save the not-so-healthy foods for the weekend or special occasions. But make sure that the not-so-healthy foods are not lying around to tempt you on Monday morning.

- **Make a list of why you are going to change to healthier eating habits and keep it handy, preferably on view at all times.** Attractively designed notices on the fridge and food cupboard doors are a good idea, with perhaps a note in your purse or wallet. Make sure your reasons are for yourself – controlling your appetite and cravings, improving energy levels, feeling healthier – and try not to focus only on weight-related reasons.

SNACKING
TO LOSE WEIGHT

LESS-THAN-1-MINUTE SKINNY SNACKS

SAVOURY

- Flavoured mini **rice cakes or rice crackers**
- **Cheese dippers**
- Low-fat **pretzels**
- Savoury **potato grills**
- **Pasta snacks**
- Low-fat **instant soups,** with or without noodles
- **Beetroot** in vinegar (jar or carton)
- **Bean salad** (jar or box)
- **Baked beans**
- Canned **sweetcorn**
- **Crispbreads** dipped in fat-free cottage cheese
- Canned or fresh **asparagus** dipped in reduced-calorie mayonnaise mixed with fat-free yoghurt
- **Vegetable crudités** dipped in low-fat cottage cheese or tzatziki
- **Sliced cooked chicken or turkey** (make sure there is no skin or visible fat)
- **Crab sticks** (can be stored in the freezer and easily defrosted in the microwave)

> **INTERESTING INFORMATION**
>
> Pretzels are considered to be one of the world's oldest snack foods and are said to have originated around 610 AD in France and Italy. The shape of pretzels is reputedly meant to represent the crossed arms of children in prayer, and monks gave pretzels to children as a reward for learning their prayers. The pretzels are baked and then dried rather than fried, which is the reason why they are considered to be a fairly healthy snack.

SWEET

- **Wine or fruit gums, boiled sweets**. Most sweets are fat free (excluding chocolates and toffees), but they contain Calories and should be eaten in moderation and counted as part of your daily carbohydrate quota.
- **Marshmallows** (3 = 1 portion of carbohydrate)
- **Nougat**
- **Liquorice sweets** (4 = 1 portion of carbohydrate)
- Fat-free **fruit or plain yoghurt**. Freeze long-life yoghurts for a frozen treat – they become quite hard, which is great as they take at least 20 minutes to eat.
- Fat-free **plain yoghurt** with a dash of vanilla extract
- Low-fat **frozen yoghurt**
- **Canned fruit** in juice with low-fat custard (instant)
- **Fresh fruit**
- **Dried fruit** – plain, bars or rolls
- **Grapes** dipped in lemon yoghurt
- **Milk shake powder** or **instant malted milk** made with cold skimmed milk
- Ice-cold glass of **skimmed milk**
- Low-fat **ice-cream** in a cone
- **Sorbet**
- Fruit **ice lollies**
- Reduced-fat **chocolate mousse** (1 small tub = 1 portion of carbohydrate)
- **Hot cross bun** plain, toasted or with fat-free cottage cheese
- Low-fat sweet **biscuits** or wafers – any biscuit with less than 1.5 g fat per biscuit (3 = 1 portion)
- Sweet **pretzels**
- Low-fat **breakfast cereals** (less than 5 g fat/100 g, preferably high-fibre) with skimmed milk
- Low-fat **health bars** (cereal-based)
- 1 Tbsp (15 ml) **oat bran** mixed in low-fat or fat-free yoghurt

DID YOU KNOW?

Dried fruit was a very important part of the diet of overland travellers and of ships' passengers and crews as it was used to help prevent scurvy. Dried fruit is a concentrated form of energy as approximately 80 g of fresh fruit is used to make 10 g dried fruit. Dried fruit is very high in fibre, with apricots being the highest. Try freezing some dried fruit to add a cooling dimension.

1–5-MINUTE SNACKS

SAVOURY

- **Sandwiches, snackwiches, crispbreads, rolls or bagels** with low-fat toppings (see pages 32–34)
- A **boiled egg** served with toast cut into soldiers – use tomato sauce as a spread
- Use **ricotta cheese** instead of mozzarella and make a salad using the ricotta, sliced tomato and fresh basil leaves. Drizzle with a little pesto and balsamic vinegar.
- **Cucumber salad** (see recipe, page 105)
- Two-minute **noodle tuna salad**: Crumble raw two-minute noodles over your tuna or chicken salad and sprinkle with lemon juice and balsamic vinegar (the noodles are not really raw, they are cooked and dehydrated). The noodles add a delicious crunchiness to the salad.
- **Basil pesto pasta** in two minutes: Cook low-fat two-minute noodles according to packet instructions, but throw away the sachet. Once cooked, mix 2 tsp (10 ml) pesto with the noodles and serve. Or, omit the pesto and toss with low-fat or fat-free cottage cheese, chopped chives and cherry tomatoes, or add tuna mixed with pickled peppers and fresh herbs.
- **Instant mashed potato** sachets (plain or flavoured): just add hot water or make your own mashed potatoes (see recipe, page 114)
- **Soft tortillas** with salsa (microwave for 20 seconds)
- **Popcorn**: microwave flavoured popcorn or make your own (see recipe, page 116)
- **Microwaved poppadums** (see cooking instructions, page 111) dipped in low-fat or fat-free cottage cheese
- **Low-fat snack meal** (200 g)
- **Hot dog** made with a low-fat frankfurter and served in a roll with tomato sauce and mustard
- **Coleslaw**: buy grated carrot and cabbage and mix with low-fat mayonnaise, fat-free plain yoghurt, a little mustard and chopped parsley and a handful of raisins
- Carton or ready-made, prepacked **fresh soup** with toast: choose soup that has less than 1 g of fat per 100 g soup or less than 3 g per 250 ml (1 cup)

- Leftover **low-fat dinner** from the night before
- Leftover **lean savoury mince** on toast
- Canned **fish** on toast (fish in brine or tomato sauce rather than oil)
- Fresh **mango** cut into chunks and dipped in a mixture of curry powder and salt

SWEET

- Fresh **strawberries and meringues**
- **Instant malted milk** made with hot skimmed milk, with a couple of marshmallows on top
- Skinny **cappuccino or café latte** with a biscotti
- Low-fat **syrup waffles (toasted)**, plain or with low-fat ice-cream
- Hot skimmed milk **with a tot of brandy or whisky** and a teaspoon of honey
- Home-made **popcorn** (see recipe, page 116) dipped in honey or syrup or sprinkled with icing sugar
- **Instant porridge** (natural = 1 portion of carbohydrate; flavoured = 2 portions of carbohydrate)

JUST-OVER-5-MINUTE SNACKS

SAVOURY

- **Baked potato** topped with ½ can of tuna, chopped tomato and lemon juice mixed with fat-free plain yoghurt or low-fat or fat-free cottage cheese or fromage frais and garnished with fresh coriander.
- **Potato salad** made with unpeeled baby potatoes and reduced-calorie mayonnaise mixed with buttermilk and chopped chives
- **Scrambled egg** (see recipe, page 115) on wholemeal toast
- **French toast**: Soak bread in egg mixture (1–2 eggs, fat-free milk, Tabasco, salt and pepper) and then pop under a hot grill. Serve with grilled tomato halves.
- **Pizza** bases with a sprinkling of feta, spinach and garlic
- **Pita bread** stuffed with low-fat

30

hummus (ready-made or home-made, see recipe page 107) and salad

- **Pita bread** stuffed with stir-fried chicken or beef strips – stir-fried in a non-stick pan with a little soy sauce – and tzatziki
- **Pancakes** (see recipe, page 117) with low-fat or fat-free cottage cheese, spinach and mushrooms
- **Home-made soup** (see recipes, pages 100–103) with cheesy croûtons (toast a slice of bread; mix 1 tsp (5 ml) grated mature Cheddar or Parmesan with 1 Tbsp (15 ml) cream cheese and spread on toast; sprinkle with paprika and place under the grill until lightly browned; cut into croûtons)
- **Chinese stir-fry** – stir-fry using soy sauce, sherry or fruit juice and a stir-fry pack of vegetables and two-minute noodles (throw the noodles in raw and discard the sachet)
- **Hamburger** made with lean mince or a grilled chicken breast burger – great with a little peri-peri sauce or reduced calorie mayonnaise
- **Corn on the cob** – plain, salted or with a little low-fat spread
- **Macaroni cheese**: Cook macaroni according to packet instructions. Once cooked, pour over made-up packet cheese sauce or reduced-fat cheese sauce from a carton, or make your own (see page 107). Serve with slices of tomato.

SWEET

- **Fruit salad** (fresh or canned in juice, not syrup) with low-fat frozen or fresh yoghurt
- **Jelly and low-fat custard** (instant or made according to box instructions with skimmed milk)
- **Smoothies** (see recipes, pages 120–123)
- **Baked apple** stuffed with raisins and cinnamon and served with low-fat custard – can be baked in oven or microwaved
- Low-fat **rusks** (see recipe, page 118)
- **Crumpets** with honey or syrup
- 1 slice low-fat **fruit cake** (see recipe, page 119)
- **Pancakes** with lemon juice and cinnamon sugar (see recipe, page 117)

LOW-FAT SANDWICH FILLERS OR CRISPBREAD TOPPINGS

Choose crispbreads that have less than 0.5 g fat per crispbread or breads that have less than 1 g fat per slice. Most breads are low in fat, including bagels, ciabatta, French loaf, seedloaf and pita bread so do not worry about searching for special low-fat breads. Make sandwiches, toast or snackwiches (use non-stick spray only if necessary) and choose from the following toppings.

REPLACEMENTS FOR BUTTER OR MARGARINE

- Use low-fat or fat-free **sieved cottage cheese** or fromage frais as a spread
- Use a low-fat spread
- If you have high cholesterol, use **unsaturated margarine in a tub (rapeseed or olive oil margarine)**
- Use **mustard or reduced-calorie mayonnaise or oil-free salad dressings** for meat, chicken, tuna or egg sandwiches
- Use **pickles or chutney** for cheese sandwiches
- If you like it hot, use a **salsa or chilli spread**

VEGETARIAN TOPPINGS AND FILLINGS

- **Yeast extract spread (Marmite)**
- **Jam, honey, syrup or marmalade**
- **Sandwich spread** (thinly spread) with lettuce and tomato
- Low-fat **peanut butter**
- **Mashed banana** – on top of yeast extract spread (Marmite) or sprinkled with cinnamon

TIP

Keep sliced bread in the freezer for extra convenience and for emergencies. Slap your filling straight onto the frozen bread and store in a lunchbox – a few hours later, you have a perfect (defrosted) sandwich.

- Canned **asparagus** with lettuce and a dash of reduced-calorie mayonnaise
- **Pineapple** ring
- Sliced **tomato** (raw or cooked) with fresh basil leaves
- **Cucumber** slices with sprouts or watercress
- **Baked beans** on toast – add finely chopped fresh chilli for spice or chopped fresh basil leaves
- **Sweetcorn** with chopped pickled peppers on toast
- **Tofu** with slices of tomato and fresh basil leaves
- Mashed **avocado** with lemon juice and black pepper – make the avocado go further by adding some fat-free cottage cheese
- **Guacamole** (see recipe, page 106)
- **Tzatziki** (see recipe, page 109) or bought
- **Hummus** (see recipe, page 107) – thinly spread if not home-made

DAIRY TOPPINGS AND FILLINGS
- **Low-fat sweet spreads** (vanilla, chocolate, strawberry) – great for kids
- **Fat-free fromage frais or cottage cheese** – add pickles or some chilli jam or turmeric
- **Fat-free fromage frais or cottage cheese** mixed with finely chopped spring onions, walnuts and celery
- **Fat-free cottage cheese** or fromage frais with chopped dried apricots and 1 tsp (5 ml) sunflower seeds
- **Crumbled feta** and very finely sliced olives or fig preserve
- Grated extra-mature **Cheddar cheese** (it has a strong flavour, therefore you only need a small amount) with cucumber slices, mango pickle (atchar) and fresh coriander leaves
- Low-fat processed **cheese spread or wedges**

> **INTERESTING INFORMATION**
>
> Processed cheese is not a very popular cheese as many people believe that it must be very 'processed'. The only extra processing this cheese goes through, however, is that the manufacturers add water and emulsifying salts (these enable fat and water to combine) to regular cheese to give it a spreadable consistency. This process reduces the fat content of the cheese and makes it a tasty yet low-fat cheese substitute for the yellow cheese fan.

- **Ricotta cheese** with chutney
- **Low-fat or fat-free cottage cheese**, banana slices, honey and sprouts

FISH, POULTRY OR MEAT TOPPINGS AND FILLINGS

- **Meat extract spread (Bovril) or stock cubes**
- **Anchovy or fish paste** – delicious with slices of tomato and fresh coriander
- Diced **chicken breast** with fresh parsley and reduced-calorie mayonnaise – add a few slices of mango or sun-dried tomato for variety
- **Reduced-fat frankfurter sausages** with mustard or tomato sauce (a.k.a. dieter's hot dogs)
- Grilled, sliced low-fat **pork sausages**
- **Ham, beef, chicken or turkey slices** – avoid processed meats or any meat with visible fat – with mustard, relish or pickles
- **Parma ham** with rocket and sliced cherry tomatoes
- **Ham** and canned or fresh pineapple
- **Savoury lean mince**
- Canned **tuna** with chopped onion, gherkins, reduced-calorie mayonnaise and fat-free plain yoghurt
- Chopped, **boiled egg** mixed with chopped onion, gherkins, reduced- calorie mayonnaise, fat-free plain yoghurt and curry powder to taste
- **Scrambled egg** (see recipe, page 115)
- **Smoked salmon** and low-fat soft cheese with capers

HIGH-FAT (AND HIGH-CHOLESTEROL) SANDWICH SPREADS TO AVOID

- Pâtés
- Liver spread
- Polony sausage
- Processed meats
- Meats with visible fat
- Butter and hard margarines
- Regular mayonnaise

LOW-FAT OR FAT-FREE CONDIMENTS

The following condiments are usually used in such small quantities that their contribution to Calorie intake is negligible. Therefore, low-fat or low-sugar tomato sauce or chutney is generally not worth the extra cost.

- Tomato sauce
- Chutney
- HP sauce
- Worcestershire sauce
- Tabasco
- Salsa
- Chilli sauce
- Piccalilli
- Relish
- Sweet-and-sour sauce
- Mustard
- Pickles in vinegar, for example gherkins, pickled onions, pickled peppers
- Balsamic vinegar
- Fruit-flavoured vinegars
- Apple sauce or jelly
- Mint sauce or jelly
- Cranberry jelly

HIGH-FAT AND HIGH-CALORIE SNACKS TO AVOID

SAVOURY

These snacks are generally high in saturated fats, which is the fat that can result in high blood cholesterol.

- Quiche
- Pies
- Croissants
- Nuts (good for cholesterol but high in fat and Calories)
- Sausage rolls
- Hot chips (even oven chips can be high in fat)
- Crisps
- Many savoury biscuits
- Savoury muffins
- Fried fish or calamari
- Samosas (even vegetarian ones)
- Most toasted or even fresh sandwiches, especially cheese, chicken, egg or tuna mayonnaise – apart from the cheese, the margarine and mayonnaise are the killers
- Salami and similar sausage sticks
- Commercial ready-dressed salads (e.g. noodle or potato salad)

SWEET
- **Chocolates**
- **Toffees**
- Most **pastries**
- Most **cakes, biscuits and puddings**
- Many **muffins**
- Carbonated or sugary **cold drinks**, including sport drinks and fruit juice (although these are fat-free, they are very high in empty Calories)

FREE SNACKS

These snacks are very low in Calories and they can be nurturing or can help to fill a gap.

SAVOURY

- **Yeast or meat extract (Marmite or Bovril) tea**
- **Miso or consommé soups**
- Home-made low-fat **vegetable juices**
- **Low-fat instant soups**, with or without noodles
- Grilled **tomato halves** sprinkled with a pinch of Parmesan and paprika and garnished with fresh basil leaves
- **Broccoli** (raw or lightly cooked) dipped in fat-free yoghurt
- **Crudités** (from list of free vegetables, page 38) and low-fat dips
- Fill **celery** 'boats' with capers, sun-dried tomatoes, parsley and basil finely chopped together
- Cooked, raw or canned **asparagus** dipped in fat-free yoghurt
- Home-made **soups** using free vegetables from list on page 38
- **Ratatouille** – courgettes, aubergines, garlic, etc., microwaved or steamed with canned tomatoes and seasoning
- Baked **courgettes, patti pan and baby gem squash** sprayed with olive oil spray and lightly seasoned

SWEET

- Diabetic **jelly**
- Frozen **lollies** made with artificially sweetened cold drink
- **Lemon or lime** frappé artificially sweetened

FREE VEGETABLES

The following vegetables are generally very low in Calories due to their high fibre and water content. They are rich in vitamins and minerals and will help to fill you up, so eat as much as you want. Try to eat at least three different kinds a day. Use these vegetables to fill up before going out for dinner, as a starter to your meal to take the edge off your hunger or as an anytime snack.

- Asparagus, artichokes
- Broccoli, cauliflower
- Celery, fennel
- Brussels sprouts, cabbage
- Spinach, watercress
- Lettuce and other salad leaves, cucumber (fresh or gherkins), radish
- Spring onions, onions, leeks
- Tomatoes, peppers, aubergines
- Marrows, squash, courgettes
- Green beans, mangetout
- Mushrooms
- Bok choy, Chinese leaves
- Beansprouts
- Chicory, Belgian endive, rocket

LOW-FAT COOKING SAUCES

Use these low-fat cooking sauces to sauté or roast vegetables, chicken, meat, etc.

- **Soy sauce** (soy and honey is my favourite basting sauce)
- Most **sweet-and-sour sauces** are low in fat
- **Sherry**
- **Wine**
- **Fruit juices**
- **Orange juice with mustard and tarragon or thyme**
- **Vegetable juices**
- **Sweet Thai chilli sauce**
- **Instant cooking sauces** – if the sauce has less than 3 g fat per portion that you are planning to consume, then it is acceptable
- **Oyster or fish sauce**

LOW-FAT WAYS TO ADD FLAVOUR

Use these low-fat ideas to add flavour before grilling, baking or sautéing vegetables, chicken, meat, etc.

- Make a **spice rub** by mixing ground spices (cumin, cardamom, coriander, chilli, paprika) with dried herbs and chopped garlic
- Make a **yoghurt marinade** by mixing natural yoghurt with herbs and spices
- Steam or bake chicken, fish or vegetables in foil packages with **fresh herbs, garlic, ginger and lemon juice**
- Sprinkle cooked food with finely chopped **sun-dried tomatoes, black olives and basil leaves**

LOW-CALORIE DRINKS

- **Plain water is best** – you need at least 6–8 glasses a day, and more if it is very hot or if you lose fluid through strenuous exercise. Keep a water bottle in your car, on your desk, in the kitchen, etc. and drink constantly.
- Dieters often believe that water fills you up and that it helps you to lose weight. Unfortunately, it is not as simple as downing a glass of water. **To fill up it is better to eat foods with a high water content**, such as fruits, vegetables, salads and soups. These will not only satisfy your appetite and the urge to eat, but are also valued for their vitamin, mineral and fibre content.
- **Water consumption does not result in increased fat or weight loss**, but it can help to prevent constipation and dehydration and keeps the body flushed of toxins. Water is vital for the absorption of food, for example, for 1 g of carbohydrate to be absorbed, it needs to bind with 3 g of water.

- **Some people seem to eat when in fact they are thirsty.** If you suspect this may apply to you, drink a couple of glasses of water before eating something and see if you are still hungry.
- **One of the most aggravating factors for constipation is insufficient fluid intake** (rather than just insufficient fibre). Those with constipation often take in plenty of fibre but not enough water. Fibre helps with constipation by acting like a sponge – it absorbs water and swells and thereby stimulates motility in the bowel. However, if there is insufficient water, the fibre can't swell and often results in worse constipation.
- **It is a common fallacy that by drinking water with your meal, you will dilute the stomach juices, which will have a negative impact on your digestion.** This is not true, as water can easily bypass any food in your stomach without affecting digestion. The only people who should be wary of drinking fluid with their meals are those suffering from indigestion, hiatus hernia, reflux or those with small appetites who need to gain weight.

- **Tomato juice** (2 cans = 1 portion of carbohydrate)
- Some **flavoured waters** – avoid those that have added sugar
- Hot or cold **water** served with fresh lemon or herbs
- **Iced tea**
- **Diet fizzy drinks**

- Artificially sweetened cordials
- Quarter **fruit juice** topped up with water or soda – drink more fruit juice if you are not able to consume 3–5 fresh fruits a day, although fresh fruit is best

> **INTERESTING INFORMATION**
>
> **Artificial sweeteners are safe** (aspartame included) if consumed in moderation. That is, no more than 6–8 sweeteners a day. Count in artificially sweetened drinks and yoghurts too.

- 1–2 heaped tsp (7.5–15 ml) **low-fat hot chocolate** drink powder with boiling water
- 1–2 heaped tsp (7.5–15 ml) **malted milk powder** with hot skimmed milk
- **Vegetable juices** diluted with water
- **Skinny cappuccinos, coffees, teas or café lattes** (a maximum of 4 cups a day)

ALCOHOL

- **White wine spritzer** (dry white wine topped up with soda and ice)
- **Beer shandy** (lite beer with diet lemonade)

> **INTERESTING INFORMATION**
>
> - **Alcohol is fat free, but it causes a drop in blood sugar, which results in hunger and cravings.** Beer drinkers are generally overweight because of what they eat when they drink, i.e. peanuts, chips, late-night munchies, hangover greasy breakfast, etc.
> - **Alcohol, however, does contain Calories and therefore needs to be moderated if you are on a Calorie-restricted eating plan for weight loss.** When drinking alcohol, your body uses the Calories from the alcohol before using the Calories from consumed food. If consuming mixed drinks (e.g. vodka and lemonade), rather choose diet mixers than the regular mixer and substitute alcohol for carbohydrate at your next meal. For example, if having a couple of glasses of wine with your meal, have only fish or chicken, salad and vegetables and leave out the potato, pasta or rice.
> - **Health guidelines recommend no more than two alcoholic beverages a day for women and no more than three a day for men.**
> - **1 alcoholic beverage = 1 glass (125 ml) white or red wine OR 1 tot (25 ml) spirits OR half a beer OR half a cider**
> - **Drink one glass of water for every drink you have** – it will slow you down and will help prevent a hangover.
> - See the section on page 48 for snacking for hangover prevention.

LATE-NIGHT SNACKING

Avoid food and drinks that contain caffeine or other stimulants, such as Coke, Diet Coke, energy drinks, tea or coffee, cocoa, hot chocolate or chocolates. High-fat snacks late at night may cause sleep disturbances as the body takes many hours to digest fat. If you often wake up during the night feeling hungry, you would definitely benefit from eating a snack that has a low GI (see page 19) just before going to sleep. Other great late-night snacks include the following:

- **1 Tbsp (15 ml) oat bran in yoghurt**
- **Hot skimmed milk drinks** such as instant malted milk
- **Fat-free or low-fat yoghurt**
- **Diet jelly and custard**
- **Free vegetable soups** (instant or home-made)
- **Decaffeinated (or herbal) tea or coffee** with low-fat sweet biscuits or biscotti
- **Hot toddy** (boiling water, dash of whisky, lemon juice, fresh ginger)
- **Hot milk with honey**

SNACKING WHEN OUT

GENERAL TIPS

- Always ask for **salad dressing and sauces on the side, or leave them out completely**.
- If you **request no dressing or sauce** and your food arrives at the table swimming in dressing, send your meal back. You are paying for it and it is your right to do so.
- Ask for your meal to be prepared **without oil, cream or butter**. Tell the waitron you are allergic to oil and see how seriously they take you.
- **Avoid sauces and gravies**. If your meal arrives covered in sauce, eat the meat, rice, etc. and try to leave as much of the sauce behind as possible.
- Health-related lies don't count. If you're at a dinner party, **refuse dessert** on the basis of an upset stomach, watching your cholesterol or feeling overfull; don't give weight-related reasons, as you will make your fellow diners feel guilty, which will result in them trying to corrupt you.
- **Never tell friends or family that you are trying to lose weight;** if you do, you will have to live up to their expectations as well as your own (plus they will scrutinize everything that you eat).
- **A peppermint after your meal takes away your desire for dessert** (as does brushing your teeth).
- **Make sure you're not starving hungry before going out to eat.**
- **If you know you are going somewhere where you are going to be tempted to eat unhealthy snacks, then either eat before you go** or, if possible, take healthy choices along with you so that you don't feel deprived and have to rely on willpower.
- **Decide before you go out that you are not going to be tempted, no matter what**. If my clients say to me that they will see what's there, we both know they will find a reason to justify why they should cheat. Once you have made up your mind that no matter what happens, you won't cheat, things are easy. The hard part is making up your mind.
- **Try to plan what you will eat before you arrive at a restaurant**. This way it will be much easier to resist peer pressure and tempting smells when it comes to placing your order.

43

SKINNY SNACKING IN RESTAURANTS

SWEET

- **Skinny cappuccino, tea, hot chocolate**, etc.
- **Bran or fruit muffin** served without jam, butter or cheese – choose low-fat muffins if available
- **Toast with a thin spreading of jam or honey** – no butter or margarine
- **Scone with jam** – no butter or cream
- **Biscotti**
- **Meringues** – plain or with fruit, no cream
- **Fruit tart**
- **Pancake** with cinnamon, sugar and lemon juice
- **Crème caramel**
- **Baked apples**
- **Pears poached in wine or fruit juice**
- **Fruit salad**, plain or with yoghurt or sorbet
- **Fruit kebabs**
- **Sorbet**
- **Frozen yoghurt**

SAVOURY

- **Anchovy toast** (delicious with sliced tomato) – no butter or margarine
- **Toast** with cottage cheese
- **Sushi**
- **Fresh oysters**
- **Ham, beef or chicken sand-wich, ciabatta, pita or roll** with mustard and salad – no butter or mayonnaise
- **Salads without dressings** – use balsamic vinegar
- **Plain or garlic pizza bread** (ask for minimal oil) – delicious with a light sprinkling of feta, tomato slices and fresh basil
- **Baked potato** with low-fat or fat-free cottage cheese, or with spinach and feta
- **Pancake** with spinach and feta, or with cottage cheese
- Scrambled, poached or boiled **eggs** with unbuttered toast
- **Soup and a bread roll** – avoid cream-based soups and ask for no cream garnish. A consommé or miso soup is a good choice.

> **INTERESTING INFORMATION**
>
> Ordering grilled fish in a restaurant is a healthy, low-fat option providing the fish is cooked with little or no fat, and is not served topped with butter or a sauce. Also make sure the vegetables are cooked without fat and are served plain without butter or sauce.
>
> When you go out for coffee, you may resist the chocolate cake, but the healthier option of a bran muffin might still have lots of fat in it and the coffee will most likely be served with full-cream milk. This means that you are still taking in fat even when ordering wisely. Therefore it is vital that you cut out hidden fats whenever you can.

SKINNY TAKE-AWAYS THAT CAN BE EATEN ON THE RUN

- **Frozen yoghurt**
- Large, freshly **baked pretzels** (breadzel)
- **Popcorn**
- **Hamburger** without sauce or chips – you can have tomato sauce
- Flame-grilled **chicken burger** without mayonnaise

TIP

Many take-away establishments don't have low-fat options like cottage cheese, and chicken, tuna and egg are often premixed with mayonnaise. However, a low-fat option that is always available, is ham and salad with mustard.

- **Pizza** without cheese – have low-fat toppings such as a light sprinkling of feta, spinach, ham, pineapple, chicken, sun-dried tomatoes, olives, banana, seafood, tuna, onion, peppers or garlic
- Low-fat **coleslaw**
- Low-fat **snack meals**
- **Sandwiches** with one protein filling (e.g. just cheese or ham – not both) and salad – ask for no margarine or mayonnaise
- **Cheese rolls or bagels** – these are baked with a sprinkling of cheese on top and are delicious on their own without filling
- **Sushi**
- **Hot cross buns**

SKINNY SNACKING AT THE MOVIES

- **Popcorn** – share a box
- **Wine gums** – share with a friend or take half the box home
- **Bottled water or diet cold drink**

WEIGHT LOSS TIP

FOR THE FREQUENT MOVIE-GOER

Choose popcorn or wine gums and leave out the carbohydrate at the previous or next meal to compensate for them.

SKINNY SNACKING AT BARBECUES

- **Garlic pizza breads**: pizza base with garlic and herbs
- **Whole mushrooms**, courgettes, baby squash sliced in half, patti pans: toss in soy sauce, garlic and seasoning and flame grill or make a basting sauce of reduced-calorie mayonnaise and chutney
- **Crudités or crispbreads** with low-fat dips (see recipes, pages 106–109)
- **Cherry tomatoes** tossed with a few olives and fresh basil leaves and drizzled with a little balsamic vinegar
- **Corn-on-the-cob** roasted on the grid: baste with a mixture of a little olive oil, lemon juice and finely chopped fresh chillies
- **Marshmallows** grilled over the flames
- **Low-fat chips** or pretzels

SKINNY SNACKING AT FOOTBALL

- Air-popped **popcorn** (see recipe, page 116)
- **Lite beers or beer shandies** made with diet lemonade
- Microwaved **poppadums** with low-fat or fat-free cottage cheese dip (see dip recipes, pages 106–109 or use instant dip sachets)
- **Sausage rolls** made with low-fat pork sausages or chicken sausage (no margarine, but go wild with mustard and tomato sauce)
- **Potato skins** (see recipe, page 113) and low-fat dip
- **Low-fat chips or pretzels**

> **TIP**
> Many butchers will make low-fat sausages on request using only lean mince and spices to fill the sausage casing.

SKINNY SNACKING AT DRINKS OR COCKTAIL PARTIES – ATTENDING OR HOSTING

- **Prunes or pineapple chunks** wrapped in low-fat bacon and baked in a moderate oven until the bacon is cooked
- **Celery sticks** filled with spicy low-fat soft cheese
- **Phyllo pastry tartlets** (see recipe, page 110)
- **Asparagus and ham wraps**
- **Ham and pineapple sticks**
- **Chicken/beef/pork satay or mini kebabs**
- **Mini pizzas**: buy mini bases and add a little strong-flavoured cheese (mature cheddar, blue cheese, feta) and vegetables
- Low-fat **dips and crispbreads or crudités** (see dip recipes, page 106–109)
- **Fish pâté** made with fat-free cottage cheese or fromage frais
- **Smoked salmon** and low-fat soft cheese on French loaf slices
- **Rice crackers** with low-fat soft cheese, garnished with chilli jam or caviar
- **Eggs** stuffed with curry-flavoured reduced-calorie mayonnaise
- Canned **smoked mussels or oysters** on crispbreads – drain oil
- Fresh **strawberries on toothpicks** with cottage cheese dip (flavour the cottage cheese with a little sugar and lemon juice)
- A bowl of plain, **fresh strawberries** goes well with champagne

SKINNY SNACKING FOR HANGOVERS

PREVENTION
- Take **multivitamins** specially designed for preventing hangovers.
- There is some validity in the old wives tale about **having an oily meal before drinking** to line your stomach, as the oily meal should slow down the absorption of the alcohol and you will therefore feel 'tipsy' later rather than sooner. However, this may not be such a good thing as you may feel so sober that you end up drinking more!
- **Drink one glass of water for every alcoholic beverage you consume**. This will keep you running to the bathroom, which reduces your drinking time and keeps you sufficiently hydrated.

CURE
- **Water** and more water – dehydration is the main culprit for making you feel bad the next morning.
- **Frequent snacks** will help to settle an uneasy stomach and stabilize blood sugars.
- Instead of a greasy breakfast, which will only help temporarily, try **scrambled eggs** with grilled tomato and bacon.
- Apart from drinking lots of caffeine-free fluids (caffeine is a diuretic and will aggravate the dehydration), eat **foods that have a high water content**. For example:
  - **Smoothies** (see recipes, pages 120–123)
  - **Fresh fruit**
  - **Salads and vegetables**
- **Fruit juice and sports drinks** are better than Coke as Coke contains caffeine
- **Multivitamin tablets** which dissolve in water
- **Rehydration sachet** or make your own rehydration drink (1 tsp (5 ml) salt, 8 tsp (40 ml) sugar, 4 cups (1 litre) cold water)

SKINNY SNACKING IN THE OFFICE – SNACKS THAT CAN BE KEPT IN A DRAWER OR HANDBAG FOR EMERGENCIES

- Low-fat **cheese wedges**
- **Dried fruit, fruit rolls or fruit bars**
- **Crispbreads**
- Low-fat **cereal or fruit bars**
- Long-life **skimmed milk** (250 ml convenience pack) – for coffee, tea or cereal
- Low-fat **breakfast cereals or porridge**
- **Yeast or meat extract spreads (Marmite or Bovril)**
- Flavoured **instant mashed potato** sachets (1 sachet = 2 portions of carbohydrate)
- **Low-fat instant soups**, with or without noodles
- **Meal replacement powder** mixed with water or skimmed milk

SKINNY SNACKING AT TEAS, BOOK CLUB OR BRIDGE – ATTENDING OR HOSTING

- **Meringues** (all unfilled meringues are fat-free)
- **Cucumber and fat-free fromage frais or low-fat soft cheese sandwiches**
- **Fat-free fruit cake** (see recipe, page 119)
- **Quiche** (see recipe, page 111)
- Low-fat **muffins or biscuits**

SKINNY SNACKS FOR TRAVELLING

CAR

- **Fresh fruit**
- **Dried fruit** snack packs or fruit bars
- **Boiled sweets**
- **Bottled water**
- **Cheese dippers**
- **Tuna snack pack**
- Packet or can of a **light meal**
- If ordering a take-away from a roadside restaurant, the safest is to order a **ham and tomato or cheese and tomato sandwich, NOT HAM AND CHEESE (toasted or fresh) without margarine or mayonnaise**, or order toast with anchovy or jam
- **Meal replacement powder** mixed with water

AEROPLANE

- **Puffed rice and marshmallow** bar
- **Fruit bars**
- Ask your air hostess for an extra **roll and cheese** (or jam) or for extra fruit salad if there are any spares available
- **Tomato cocktail** without the vodka
- Pre-order **low-fat or low-cholesterol meals** through your travel agent – most airlines have these available
- **Meal replacer** mixed with water

- If possible, and especially if you have a medical condition, it is advisable to **consult a registered dietician** to have an individualized plan worked out for you. The plans given in this section are generalized and may not work for everyone.
- Variety is the secret to both physical and mental health so use the eating plans as guidelines only and try to **vary your intake** as much as possible on a daily basis (see exchange lists on pages 53–57).
- **Have tea and coffee with skimmed milk** and limit your intake to four cups a day; if you drink herbal teas, you can have more.
- **Use salt sparingly**. As a rule, use salt only for cooking and avoid using it at the dinner table.
- Try to **limit your sugar intake** to 4 tsp (20 ml) a day. If you need to use more sugar and you are either diabetic or trying to lose weight, then it may be a good idea to use artificial sweeteners, but limit the sweeteners to 6–8 a day.
- Try to **drink 6–8 glasses** of water a day.
- **Try to limit drinking alcohol to weekends only** and try to have no more than three (men) or two drinks (women) a day. If you are trying to lose weight, substitute the alcohol for the carbohydrate at that meal. In other words, if you have a couple of glasses of wine with your meal, just have the fish or meat and lots of salad and vegetables, and leave out the potatoes, pasta or rice.

IDEAL
EATING PLANS

WEIGHT-LOSS GUIDELINES

- **Eat 5–6 meals or snacks a day**; don't skip any of these.

- **Plan ahead** and make provision for emergencies (see shopping list, page 97).

- Have **three fat portions** from the good fat list (see page 57) spread throughout the day, except when eating out (where you will more than likely be consuming hidden fats) or knowingly taking in excess fats. Remember that a totally fat-free diet is unnecessary and unhealthy.

- **Red meat** can be eaten a maximum of three times a week. Use lean cuts only, and when possible use game which is very low in fat.

- **Eat only 3–4 eggs a week**. The cholesterol and fat is in the yolk, so if you want to stretch out your eggs, then use extra whites.

- **Use free vegetables (page 55) to fill you up**. It is often useful to start your meal with free vegetables in the form of salad, soup, crudités or grilled vegetables. Doing this will ensure that you are satisfied with a smaller portion of your main course.

- Spread your **fruit and carbohydrate portions** throughout the day.

- Everyone should have the equivalent of **two to three portions of dairy** a day (see page 53). Pregnant or breastfeeding women and growing children may need four portions a day. If you are unable to have dairy for any reason, it may be necessary to take calcium supplements. A dietician will be able to assess your intake and requirements and advise you on non-dairy sources of calcium.

- **Cook without oil or other fat**; instead use soy sauce, wine, chutney, tomato sauce and stock. You can also use spices, herbs, curry powders, etc. See pages 98–99 for low-fat cooking tips.

FOOD EXCHANGES

The food exchanges that follow enable you to create your own eating plan according to your likes and dislikes. The eating plans on pages 58–65 indicate the appropriate number of exchanges to choose from each food group. Try to work around those numbers on a daily basis.

DAIRY GROUP

1 SERVING

= 1 cup (250 ml) skimmed milk (long-life or fresh)

= 25 g (60 ml) skimmed milk powder

= ¾ cup (200 ml) buttermilk

= 1 small tub (175 ml) fat-free fruit/plain yoghurt

CARBOHYDRATE GROUP

BREADS AND ROLLS

= 1 slice bread (30 g),
cut 1 cm thick

= Half a roll, bagel or pita

= Half a hot cross bun

CRACKERS

= 2 crispbreads
(wholemeal) or
cream crackers

= 2 rice cakes

= ½ matzos or 5 water
biscuits

= 4 thin Swedish crisp
breads

CEREALS

= ½ cup (125 ml) cooked
porridge

= ¾ cup (200 ml) bran,
cereal or cornflakes

= 1 wheat cereal biscuit

= 1 cup (250 ml) puffed,
unsweetened cereal

= ⅓ cup (80 ml) low-fat
muesli

RICE AND PASTA

= ½ cup (125 ml) cooked
rice or pasta

= ½ cup cooked couscous

STARCHY VEGETABLES

= 1 medium potato

= ½ cup (125 ml) mashed
potato

= 1 medium sweetcorn or 5
Tbsp (75 ml) sweetcorn

= 1 cup (250 ml) beetroot,
squash, carrots, peas
or pumpkin

= 1 cup (250 ml) thick
vegetable soup

LEGUMES

= ½ cup (125 ml) dried beans,
peas, lentils – cooked

= 5 Tbsp (75 ml) baked beans

= 1 cup (250 ml) thick soup

ALCOHOL

= 1 glass (125 ml) dry white
or red wine

= 1 tot (25 ml) spirits

= ½ can beer or cider

OCCASIONAL TREATS

= 1 tube wine gums

= 4 boiled sweets

= 1 Tbsp (15 ml) jam or honey

= 1 scoop low-fat or fat-free
ice-cream

= 1 rusk or small bran muffin

= 3 low-fat sweet biscuits

= 1½ cups (375 ml) popcorn

FRUIT GROUP

1 SERVING 1 SERVING 1 SERVING 1 SERVING 1 SERVING

FRESH FRUIT

= 1 apple, banana or pear

= 1 orange or grapefruit

= 1 peach or nectarine

= 1 small mango or
  1 kiwi fruit

= 15 (1 cup) grapes or
  cherries

= ⅓ small melon or a large
  slice of watermelon

= 3 slices pineapple

= 2 apricots, plums or figs

= 2 guavas

= 1 cup papaya or
  strawberries

= 12 lychees

= ¾ cup fruit salad

DRIED FRUIT

= 5 apple rings

= 2 peach or pear halves

= 3 prunes or 20 raisins
  (large tablespoon)

= 4 apricot halves or dates

FRUIT JUICE

= ½ cup (125 ml) unsweetened
  fruit juice

FREE VEGETABLES

Eat as much as you want, in soups, salads, stir-fries or as crudités.
Try to eat at least three different kinds a day.

- Asparagus, artichokes
- Broccoli, cauliflower, celery
- Brussels sprouts, cabbage
- Spinach, lettuce, cucumber (fresh or gherkins)
- Peppers, radish, spring onions, onions
- Tomatoes, aubergines, marrows, patty pan squash
- Green beans, mange tout, gem squash, mushrooms

PROTEIN GROUP
1 SERVING = 30 g or 1 matchbox or small egg size

1 SERVING 1 SERVING 1 SERVING 1 SERVING 1 SERVING 1 SERVING 1 SERVING 1 SERVING 1 SERVING 1 SERVING

LOW-FAT PROTEIN (EAT MOST OFTEN)

= Chicken breast (no skin) (1 breast = approx. 3 servings)

= White fish – can have extra 2 servings

= Medium-fat fish (sardines, tuna, trout

= Game, veal or venison

= Turkey, pheasant or guinea fowl

= Crab, lobster or crayfish

= Oysters or mussels

= Fat-free cottage cheese or fromage frais, or or low fat
  soft cheese (2 Tbsp (30 ml) = 1 serving) or ricotta cheese
  or low-fat processed cheese (e.g. low-fat cheese
  wedges) (2 wedges = 1 serving)

= ½ cup (125 ml) dried beans, peas or lentils – cooked

MEDIUM-FAT PROTEIN (ONLY EAT 3 TIMES A WEEK)

= Red meat: pork, beef, lamb, mutton (fat trimmed)

= Liver

= Egg (no more than 3–4 egg yolks a week)

= High-fat fish (herring, mackerel, salmon)

= Low-fat hard cheese (Edam, etc.)

= 2 Tbsp (30 ml) hummus

HIGH-FAT PROTEIN (TRY TO AVOID)

= Sirloin and rump

= Pork spareribs

= Duck, goose

= Full-fat cheese (Cheddar, gruyère, emmenthal, gouda,
  roquefort, mozzarella, Parmesan, brie, camembert, feta)

= Salami, beef or pork sausage, Russian sausage

= Soya patties or sausages

FAT GROUP

GOOD FATS (HEALTHY, BUT STILL FATTENING)

= 1 tsp (5 ml) soft margarine

= 2 tsp (10 ml) low-fat spread

= 1 tsp (5 ml) vegetable oil (sunflower, olive, rapeseed)

= 2 tsp (10 ml) peanut butter

= 2 walnuts or 4 almonds

= 1 Tbsp (15 ml) sunflower seeds

= ¼ avocado

= 6 olives

POOR FATS (UNHEALTHY AND FATTENING)

= 1 tsp (5 ml) butter

= 1½ tsp (7.5 ml) medium-fat spread

= 1 tsp (5 ml) mayonnaise

= 2 tsp (10 ml) reduced-calorie or oil-free French dressing

= 1 Tbsp (15 ml) thin cream

= 1 rasher of bacon

- Skimmed milk has less fat than full-cream milk but almost the same vitamin and mineral content. Long-life skimmed milk has been heated to a very high temperature for a few seconds, which gives a creamier taste and texture and is therefore much more acceptable to those used to full-cream milk. It is a fallacy that skimmed milk has been watered down.

- The whiter the meat, the lower the fat and cholesterol content. This is why a chicken leg or thigh is tastier and juicier than the breast meat which is drier because it contains less fat. Exceptions are game such as venison and hare, which are very low in fat. Lower fat meats should not be overcooked as they will become dry.

- Low-fat soft cheese is not a low-fat product, although it is slightly lower in fat. Rather choose fat-free soft cheese.

BREAKFAST (7–8 AM)

- 2 wheat cereal biscuits OR 1½ cups low-fat cereal with skimmed milk or fat free yoghurt (fruit or plain) AND 1 fruit OR ½ glass fruit juice
- Tea or coffee with skimmed milk

MORNING SNACK (10–11 AM)

- 1 slice of toast OR 3 crispbreads with 2 Tbsp (30 ml) fat-free or low-fat cottage cheese, fish paste (with tomato slices), yeast extract spread (use low-fat margarine or fat-free cottage cheese as a spread) AND 1 fruit. OR
- Convenience option: 1 cereal bar AND 1 fruit bar

LUNCH (1–2 PM)

- 2 slices of bread OR 1 roll OR 1 large baked potato with 2 low-fat cheese wedges OR 1 slice of ham OR ⅓ of a 170 g can of tuna in brine. You can have mustard, chutney or 2 tsp (10 ml) reduced-calorie mayonnaise; AND salads with balsamic vinegar or oil-free salad dressing. OR
- Convenience option: low-fat snack meal (200 g) AND salads with balsamic vinegar or oil-free salad dressing

AFTERNOON SNACK (4–5 PM)

- 1 fat-free fruit yoghurt AND 1 fruit AND 2–3 crispbreads with ¼ avocado or 2 tsp (10 ml) peanut butter OR 3 low-fat biscuits

SUPPER (7–8 PM)

- Cooked meal with 3 matchboxes (size of 1 chicken fillet) of fish, chicken, lean meat OR 1 cup cooked legumes; AND and a large baked potato OR 1 cup of cooked rice or pasta OR 2 cups of starchy vegetables (see page 54); AND lots of free vegetables (see page 55). OR
- Convenience option: low-fat meal (300 g) AND lots of free vegetables (see page 55).

EVENING SNACK (9–11 PM)

- 1 cup skimmed milk with 2 heaped teaspoons of instant hot malted milk powder AND
  1 fruit. OR
- 1 fat-free fruit or plain yoghurt AND 1 fruit

PORTION ALLOCATION

	CARBOHYDRATE	PROTEIN	FRUIT	DAIRY	FAT
BREAKFAST	2		1	1	
MID AM	1	1	1		
LUNCH	2	1			1
MID PM	1		1	1	1
SUPPER	2	3			1
LATE PM			1	1	
TOTALS	8	5	4	3	3

BREAKFAST (7–8 AM)

- 1 wheat cereal biscuits OR ¾ cup low-fat cereal with skimmed milk or fat-free yoghurt (fruit or plain) AND 1 fruit OR ½ glass fruit juice
- Tea or coffee with skimmed milk

MORNING SNACK (10–11 AM)

- 1 slice of toast OR 3 crispbreads with a thin spreading of fat-free or low-fat cottage cheese, fish paste (with tomato slices) or yeast extract spread (use low-fat margarine or fat-free cottage cheese as a spread) AND 1 fruit. OR
- Convenience option: 1 cereal bar AND 1 fruit bar

LUNCH (1–2 PM)

- 2 slices of bread OR 1 roll OR 1 large baked potato with 2 low-fat cheese wedges OR 1 slice of ham OR ⅓ of a 170 g can of tuna in brine. You can have mustard, chutney or 2 tsp (10 ml) low-fat mayonnaise; AND salads with balsamic vinegar or oil-free salad dressing. OR
- Convenience option: low-fat snack meal (200 g) AND salads with balsamic vinegar or oil-free salad dressing

AFTERNOON SNACK (4–5 PM)

- 1 fat-free fruit yoghurt AND 1 fruit AND 2–3 crispbreads with ¼ avocado or 2 tsp (10 ml) peanut butter OR 3 crispbreads

SUPPER (7–8 PM)

- Cooked meal with 3 matchboxes (size of 1 chicken fillet) of fish, chicken, lean meat OR 1 cup cooked legumes; AND a medium baked potato OR ½ cup cooked rice or pasta OR 1 cup of starchy vegetables (see page 54); AND lots of free vegetables (see page 55). OR
- Convenience option: low-fat meal (200 g) AND lots of free vegetables (see page 55).

EVENING SNACK (9–11 PM)

- 1 cup skimmed milk with 2 heaped teaspoons of instant hot malted milk drink OR
- 1 fat-free fruit or plain yoghurt

PORTION ALLOCATION

	CARBOHYDRATE	PROTEIN	FRUIT	DAIRY	FAT
BREAKFAST	1		1	1	
MID AM	1		1		
LUNCH	2	1			1
MID PM	1		1	1	1
SUPPER	1	3			1
LATE PM				1	
TOTALS	6	4	3	3	3

61

BREAKFAST (7–8 AM)

- 2 wheat cereal biscuits OR 1½ cups low-fat cereal with skimmed milk or fat-free yoghurt (fruit or plain) AND 1 fruit OR ½ glass fruit juice
- Tea or coffee with skimmed milk

MORNING SNACK (10–11 AM)

- 2 slices of toast OR 6 crispbreads with a thin spreading of fat-free or low-fat cottage cheese, fish paste (with tomato slices) or yeast extract spread (use low-fat margarine) AND 1 fruit. OR
- Convenience option: 2 cereal bars OR 1 low-fat bar AND 1 fruit bar

LUNCH (1–2 PM)

- 2 slices of bread OR 1 roll OR 1 large baked potato with 2 low-fat cheese wedges OR 1 slice of ham OR ⅓ of a 170 g can of tuna in brine. You can have mustard, chutney or 2 tsp (10 ml) reduced-calorie mayonnaise; AND salads with balsamic vinegar or oil-free salad dressing. OR
- Convenience option: low-fat snack meal (200 g) AND salads with balsamic vinegar or oil-free salad dressing

AFTERNOON SNACK (4–5 PM)

- 1 low-fat fruit yoghurt AND 1 fruit AND 6 crispbreads with 2 Tbsp (30 ml) low-fat cottage cheese or fromage frais, ¼ avocado or 2 tsp (10 ml) peanut butter. OR
- Convenience option: Make 2 sandwiches at lunchtime and have the one at lunch and save the other for this snack

SUPPER (7–8 PM)

- Cooked meal with 4 matchboxes (size of 1½ chicken fillets) of fish, chicken, lean meat OR 1½ cups cooked legumes; AND 1 large baked potato OR 1 cup of cooked rice or pasta OR 2 cups of starchy vegetables (see page 54); AND lots of free vegetables (see page 55). OR
- Convenience option: low-fat meal (400 g) AND lots of free vegetables (see page 55)

EVENING SNACK (9–11 PM)

- 1 cup skimmed milk with 2 heaped teaspoons of instant malted milk powder AND 1 fruit AND 3 low-fat biscuits OR
- 1 low fat fruit or plain yoghurt AND 1 fruit AND 3 low-fat sweet biscuits

PORTION ALLOCATION

	CARBOHYDRATE	PROTEIN	FRUIT	DAIRY	FAT
BREAKFAST	2		1	1	
MID AM	2		1		1
LUNCH	2	1			1
MID PM	2	1	1	1	1
SUPPER	2	4			1
LATE PM	1		1	1	
TOTALS	11	6	4	3	4

BREAKFAST (7–8 AM)
- 2 wheat cereal biscuits OR 1½ cups low-fat cereal with skimmed milk or fat-free yoghurt (fruit or plain) AND 1 fruit OR ½ glass fruit juice
- Tea or coffee with skimmed milk

MORNING SNACK (10–11 AM)
- 1 slice of toast OR 3 crispbreads with a thin spreading of fat-free cottage cheese or fromage frais, fish paste or yeast extract (use low-fat margarine or low-fat cottage cheese as a spread) AND 1 fruit. OR
- Convenience option: 1 cereal bar OR 1 low-fat bar AND 1 fruit bar

LUNCH (1–2 PM)
- 2 slices bread OR 1 roll OR 1 large baked potato with 1 slice of ham OR ⅓ of a 170 g can of tuna in brine. Use mustard, chutney or 2 tsp (10 ml) reduced-calorie mayonnaise; AND salads with balsamic vinegar or oil-free salad dressing. OR
- Convenience option: low-fat snack meal (200 g) AND salads with balsamic vinegar or oil-free salad dressing

AFTERNOON SNACK (4–5 PM)
- 1 fat-free fruit yoghurt AND 1 fruit AND 2–3 low-fat biscuits with 2 low-fat cheese wedges, 2 Tbsp (30 ml) low-fat or fat-free cottage cheese, ¼ avocado or 2 tsp (10 ml) peanut butter. OR
- Convenience option: Make 2 sandwiches for your mid-morning snack and eat half at mid-morning, half at mid-afternoon and have the other one at lunch

SUPPER (7–8 PM)

- Cooked meal with 3 matchboxes (size of 1 chicken fillet) of fish, chicken, lean meat OR 1 cup cooked legumes; AND 1 large baked potato OR 1 cup of cooked rice or pasta OR 2 cups of starchy vegetables (see page 54); AND lots of free vegetables (see page 55). OR
- Convenience option: low-fat meal (300 g) AND lots of free vegetables (see page 55)

EVENING SNACK (9–11 PM)

- 1 cup skimmed milk with 2 heaped teaspoons of instant malted milk powder AND 1 fruit. OR
- 1 fat-free fruit or plain yoghurt AND 1 fruit

PORTION ALLOCATION

	CARBOHYDRATE	PROTEIN	FRUIT	DAIRY	FAT
BREAKFAST	2		1	1	
MID AM	1		1		
LUNCH	2	1			1
MID PM	1	1	1	1	1
SUPPER	2	3			1
LATE PM			1	1	
TOTALS	8	5	4	3	3

65

SNACKING TO GAIN WEIGHT

- **If your body fat is normal** (13–19% for males and 20–26% for females) and you want to gain lean or muscle weight, **you need to eat high energy and high protein snacks while limiting your fat intake**.
- **If your body fat is low** and you need to gain lean and fat weight, then **you need to eat high energy, high protein and healthy (unsaturated) fat snacks**.
- Please note that these nutritional guidelines are for those who are following an exercise programme conducive to weight gain; muscle mass cannot and will not increase without an appropriate exercise programme.
- At first, **those with smaller appetites may struggle to eat all the food required**. It is vital you eat 6 meals a day to reduce the symptoms of bloating, constipation and nausea that are common complaints at this stage. Start with slightly smaller portions and then gradually increase your portion sizes.
- As you are probably eating larger quantities of food, **it is necessary to take in more fluids than usual** in order for the body to efficiently absorb and digest the extra food. If you struggle to eat all your food, don't drink fluid with your meals as it may fill you up prematurely.

INTERESTING INFORMATION

Liquid meal supplements are generally low in fat and high in protein, vitamins, minerals and carbohydrates. They can be used by the average person as a meal replacement in emergency situations, e.g. too sick to eat, or travelling or time constraints. They should not form part of the average diet but are useful to know about for those times when a normal meal isn't possible. They could also be used as a pre-event meal for the person who can't exercise on a full stomach or as a supplement to the diet of a person trying to gain weight.

SNACKS FOR WEIGHT GAIN

- **Liquid meal supplements/replacement powders**, some of which are mixed with water while others are mixed with milk.
- **Nuts and raisins**
- Toasted, flavoured **nuts**
- **Seed bars, yoghurt bars, energy bars**
- **Peanut snack bars**
- **Smoothies** (see recipes, pages 120–123)
- **Packs of** seeds, nuts and raisins, or mix your own
- **Olives**
- **Peanut butter and honey** on toast
- **Avocado** on toast
- **Banana, apple slices or celery sticks smeared with peanut butter and dotted with raisins**
- **Baked potato with tuna and sweetcorn** – add a sprinkling of feta cheese
- **Two-minute noodles** (throw away the sachet) with pesto sauce and diced chicken fillet
- **Baked beans** on wholemeal toast (add diced low-fat frankfurters for extra protein)
- **Malted milk powder** (4 tsp/20 ml) made with 1 cup skimmed milk, 4 tsp (20 ml) skimmed milk powder and honey to taste
- **Jelly and custard** (add extra skimmed milk powder to the custard and use low-fat evaporated milk instead of water in the jelly recipe). You can buy low-fat custard or make your own (see recipe on the back of custard powder packet).
- Use **low-fat evaporated milk and skimmed milk powder** (avoid unhealthy milk powder blends) to add extra protein and Calories to milk drinks, soups, sauces, cereal, etc.
- Use **low-fat condensed milk** to add sweetness to cereal, fruit or smoothies, or sip on its own
- **Sweets, fruit, sweetened cold drinks** such as Coke, sports drinks, etc. add extra energy without adding extra fat
- **Muesli bars** or no-added-fat bars
- **Liquidize a banana, glass of milk and scoop of ice-cream with a few teaspoons of peanut butter**

67

IDEAL EATING PLAN FOR SOMEONE WHO WANTS TO GAIN **MUSCLE WEIGHT** WHILE GAINING **MINIMAL FAT WEIGHT**

TAKE NOTE:
Exact portion sizes will be determined by age, activity and metabolism.

FIRST THING

- Meal replacement drink OR smoothie made with fruit and dairy (see recipes, pages 120–123)

BREAKFAST (7–9 AM)

- 3–4 slices of toast with poached egg, fish, avocado, peanut butter or jam (use low-fat margarine or rapeseed or olive oil margarine); AND tea or coffee with milk. OR
- 2–3 cups of low-fat cereal with skimmed milk or fat-free yoghurt – use honey for sweetening
- Tea or coffee with milk
- 4 eggs a week (can have extra egg whites)

MORNING SNACK (10–11 AM)

- Fresh fruit and yoghurt AND snacks from the list on page 67

LUNCH (1–2 PM)

- 4 slices of bread OR 2–3 cups leftover pasta OR 2 rolls with your choice of peanut butter, cheese, avocado, 4 slices of ham, beef, turkey or white meat of chicken (no skin, no mayonnaise), a 170 g can of tuna in brine or low-fat cottage cheese or fromage frais. Use mustard, chutney, oil-free dressing or reduced-calorie mayonnaise and salad.

AFTERNOON SNACK (4–5 PM)

- 2 slices of bread (see previous toppings) OR 1 muffin OR 1 low-fat snack bar AND 1 fruit AND snacks from page 67

SUPPER (7–8 PM)

- Cooked meal with 5 matchboxes (2 small chicken fillets) of fish, chicken or meat AND lots of vegetables AND a large baked potato AND/OR rice or pasta. Use olive oil or other vegetable oils (rapeseed, sunflower, etc.) when cooking the meal.

EVENING SNACK

- Meal replacement drink OR smoothie AND snacks from the list on page 67

SNACKING TO MAINTAIN WEIGHT, HEALTH AND ENERGY

You should choose snacks from the weight-loss section 70% of the time and relax about the fat and energy content of your snacks 30% of the time; or eat low-fat during the week and relax at weekends. Over the years, I have studied my clients and have noticed that the main difference between my permanently successful clients and those who end up having to see me again and again, is their goals for changing their eating and lifestyle habits.

WHEN THE MAIN GOAL IS WEIGHT LOSS
(THOSE WHO CHANGE THEIR EATING HABITS TEMPORARILY
AND USUALLY LOSE WEIGHT AND REGAIN IT)

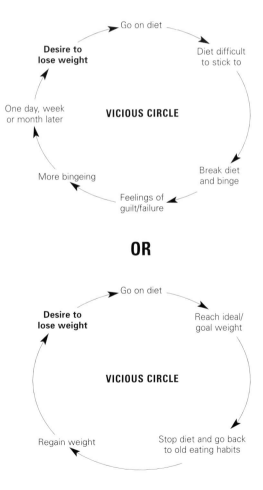

Other goals that often don't lead to permanent weight loss:

- Fit into **clothes**
- Fit into **society**
- Feel **accepted**
- Feel more **confident**
- Feel more **assertive**

People who have these goals may lose weight but can't maintain it for reasons such as disappointment (don't feel more confident, happy or accepted even when thin) or unattainable, unrealistic goals.

GOALS OF THOSE WHO CHANGE THEIR EATING HABITS PERMANENTLY AND LOSE WEIGHT AND MAINTAIN IT

- **BE** more healthy: **short term**, e.g. avoid colds and flu **long term**, e.g. prevent cancer, heart disease
- **FEEL** more **healthy**
- **Increased, consistent energy levels**
- **Appetite and craving control**
- **Stabilize blood sugars**
- **Existing medical disorder**
- **Family health and good role model for children**
- **Stop dieting and bingeing cycle**

TIP

Use these goals as reasons for refusing a certain high-fat food. Saying no to a piece of cake for blood sugar reasons is much easier than saying no for weight reasons.

SNACKING FOR SPORTS AND TRAINING

- **NB! Always test sports supplements or drinks** before relying on them in prolonged stressful situations such as competitions.
- If you are training for no more than about an hour at a time and your goal is fitness, health and weight loss, then sports drinks or supplements are probably not necessary.
- If training for over an hour at a time or your goal is mainly fitness, then sports drinks/supplements may be necessary and of benefit.
- **Consume 500–1000 ml of water per hour of exercise** – depends on heat, exercise intensity, your sweat rate, etc.
- **Your body works like a steam engine** and needs fuel (food, sports drinks and supplements) to operate efficiently.

SPORTS DRINKS

- These drinks have a high GI and are very quickly absorbed.
- **Most of the well-known brands are fairly similar so choose one that suits you.** It is recommended that you use one that appeals to you in taste and that causes no side-effects (even Coke, possibly diluted with a little water, can be used).
- **Sports drinks should be used for prolonged training and competition sessions** (e.g. generally exercising for longer than 1–2 hours). These drinks can be used before, during as well as after the exercise session for rehydration and refueling.
- **They can also be used if, for example, you are planning to go straight from an aerobic class to the shops with no time for lunch,** although this should be the exception rather than the rule. A sandwich with a bottle of water will have a much more lasting and satisfying effect, whereas a sports drink will be very quickly absorbed and will therefore provide you with instant energy, but that energy will be fairly short-lived.

VERY HIGH CARBOHYDRATE POWDERS, DRINKS OR GELS

- These are recommended for **carbo-loading just before an event**.
- **They can also be used by the heavy trainer or competitor for post-training recovery,** as well as during endurance events, where they can be diluted with water.
- **These have no use for the average gym-goer.**

PROTEIN SHAKES OR SUPPLEMENTS

- Normally used for **muscle gain**.
- **Important for those not eating enough protein or with very high protein requirements,** such as vegetarians, those growing rapidly, endurance athletes, etc.
- **The average Western diet is already high in protein.**
- **Too much protein can place strain on the kidneys.**
- **If the protein comes from an animal source, your intake of saturated fats may be too high,** which may negatively affect your cholesterol levels.

MEAL REPLACERS

- **Low in fat, balanced in protein, Calories, vitamins and minerals, meal replacers are useful for those who can't eat a proper meal** due to travel constraints or other problems such as illness.
- **Also used for weight gain** (see pages 66–67).

SPORTS BARS

- **Some sports bars are high in fat** so the weight conscious would need to choose carefully.
- **These bars are often useful due to their convenience properties** rather than their nutritional value.

INSTANT ENERGY SNACKS – HIGH GI FOODS (SEE PAGE 19)

USES

- **Carbo-loading**
- **Pre-event meal**
- **During performance**
- **These foods are quickly absorbed** and provide instant energy.
- **Because these foods are quickly absorbed, they should have minimal bloating effects** and can therefore be consumed shortly before exercising or performing. (Warning: always check your body's response to new foods under practice conditions rather than performance conditions.)

EXAMPLES

- **Sugary sweets** such as jelly tots, wine gums, vitamin C sweets
- **Fruit**, especially tropical fruit such as bananas and melon
- Puffed **rice cereal and marshmallow sweets**
- **Low-fat sports bars** (not cereal based)
- **Sports drinks**
- **Sugary cold drinks**, e.g. Coke, fruit juice
- **Sugar-sweetened, non-wholemeal breakfast cereals** such as chocolate or honey-coated or frosted cereals with skimmed milk

- **Honey, jam or syrup on toast** (no margarine or butter)
- **Mashed banana on toast**
- **Baked potato with fat-free fromage frais or cottage cheese**
- **Low-fat two-minute noodles**
- **Sweetened canned fruit**

SNACKING FOR EMOTIONAL EATERS OR THOSE EATING FOR REASONS OTHER THAN HUNGER

DO YOU OFTEN:
- **Eat even though you are not physically hungry?**
- Nearly **always feel over-full** after eating?
- **Eat when you are depressed, tired, stressed, angry, etc.?**
- **Feel that food chooses you**, rather than you choosing the food?
- **Feel regret and guilt after eating?**
- **Feel out of control when eating**, i.e. want to stop but can't?
- **Lie in bed at night planning to start an exercise programme or diet the next day?**

If you answered yes to any of the above questions, then you may be suffering from disordered eating behaviour (different from eating disorders), which normally has its roots in emotional issues.

TRY TO IDENTIFY WHY YOU NEED TO SNACK
- Try to identify whether you are eating for **stomach hunger** (real physical hunger) or **mouth hunger** (emotional hunger).
- **Mouth hunger is insatiable** – it can never be satisfied by food.
- **Mouth hunger causes bingeing and cheating.**
- **Recognizing mouth hunger will help you to see that it is not you who is weak-willed but a real emotion that is causing the binge.** This helps prevent guilt, which would normally result in more bingeing.
- **Recognizing emotions that commonly result in bingeing** will enable you to respond more appropriately to those emotions.

OTHER COMMON REASONS FOR OVEREATING

- **Eating because you are cold**: First warm yourself as food can't warm you significantly and therefore you may just continue snacking even though you are not hungry. (The body does produce heat, however, as a by-product of digestion – this is called the thermic effect of feeding and it plays a very small role in keeping your metabolism active!)
- **Make sure that you are not thirsty** – Many people eat food when in fact they should be taking in fluid as they have confused hunger and thirst signals.
- **Some people eat when they are physically tired.** For example after an exhausting gym session you may feel that you deserve to eat lots of food.

THE FOLLOWING SNACKING TIPS OR GUIDELINES CAN HELP YOU TO MANAGE YOUR EATING BETTER

- **Serotonin is a 'feel good' messenger that is released by your body after eating carbohydrates.** Eat at least 1 carbohydrate every 3 hours to keep up your serotonin levels.
- **Choose mostly from the slow-release carbohydrates** to ensure a constant release of serotonin (low GI, see page 19).
- **Eat 5–6 meals or snacks a day.**
- **Never skip a snack as this will cause you to overeat at the next meal as well as to be tempted by unhealthy foods.**
- **Get organized** so that you always have snacks at your fingertips.
- **Keep permanent snacks in your handbag, office drawer or in your car** for emergencies (see page 49).
- **Plan ahead for your meals and snacks for the day.**
- **Always ask yourself why you are about to eat something** – eating a snack to keep your blood sugars stable is good; eating a snack because you are stressed is inappropriate.
- **Keep a record of what you are eating and feeling** (especially when you feel out of control with your eating) – this will help you to keep things in perspective and help to make you feel in control. You will also be able to identify common emotions or circumstances that result in bad eating habits and thereby arm yourself with specific appropriate tools to manage those emotions or circumstances.

- **Nurture as well as nourish yourself with your snacks:**
  - **Don't eat on the run**; sit and savour your food.
  - **Never eat standing up in the kitchen**, in the car or in front of the television.
  - **Always put your snack on a plate.**
  - **Eat slowly.**
- **Forgive yourself if you binge**; feeling guilt and regret will result in more bingeing.
- **Don't feel guilty about choosing to have one slice of cake**; you chose to have that one slice. The problem occurs when two or more slices of cake choose you.
- **Find appropriate activities or responses to your emotions that work for you**, e.g. treat yourself to a massage, phone a friend, go for a walk or to gym, take up a hobby, psychotherapy, etc.

HOW SNACKING CAN HELP YOU GIVE UP SMOKING AND PREVENT WEIGHT GAIN

Many people are scared to give up smoking as they are worried that they will gain weight. In fact, many people continue smoking as they believe it helps them to manage their weight. Firstly, let's look at why people seem to gain weight when they stop smoking.

- **Smoking increases your metabolism slightly**, so when you stop smoking your metabolism decreases to its normal pre-smoking level and your weight may also increase to its pre-smoking level.
- **Smoking is a natural full stop to meals.**
- **Smoking a cigarette is often seen as a form of comfort or reward**, and many people turn to food to fulfil this role once they have given up smoking.
- **Smoking decreases your sense of taste so when you kick the habit**, food starts to taste better.
- **Smoking seems to go well with coffee**, and both nicotine and caffeine can suppress your appetite. Without this effect, you will have to learn how to manage your normal appetite.
- **Smoking results in taking in less alcohol when drinking**, so without a cigarette to smoke, you take more sips of your drink and therefore end up drinking more.

All the previous points help to explain why people gain weight when they stop smoking, but you should still not gain more than a couple of kilograms! Snacking on the right foods is essential not only to prevent weight gain, but also to help with giving up smoking. Here are some tips on preventing excessive weight gain when you decide to take that big decision.

- **Make sure your diet is adequately balanced and low in fat.** It may be necessary to see a dietician at this stage, to learn how to maintain your weight, rather than at a later stage when you have to worry about weight loss.
- **Exercise to increase your metabolism as much as possible.**
- **Create a new full stop to your meals and snacks,** for example brush your teeth, eat a peppermint, move away from the table and do the dishes, drink a glass of water, make a cup of tea, eat a piece of fruit, etc.
- **Eat smaller meals more often (5–6 meals a day) to keep your metabolism working** and your cravings under control.
- **Make sure your meals nurture as well as nourish you;** don't eat on the run or in front of the television. Concentrate on what you are eating and make your meals interesting and appealing.
- **Drink one glass of water for every alcoholic drink you consume.**
- **Have plenty of low-Calorie snacks available for when you just can't resist the urge to put something in your mouth.** This is vital during the initial stage of giving up smoking.

SNACKING FOR DIABETICS

- **If you haven't consulted a dietician or diabetic specialist about your diabetic diet, it is strongly recommended that you do so.**
- **Overweight diabetics should read through the section on weight loss as well as this section.**
- **Low GI snacks (see page 19) will help to keep your blood sugars stable** without peaks and lows.
- **High GI foods are useful if a diabetic feels hypoglycaemic** (blood sugars have dropped too low). If this occurs, a high GI snack should be taken straight away, followed by a low GI food as soon as they feel that their blood sugars have gone back up.

- **Artificially sweetened foods should generally be used** as long as no more than eight artificial sweeteners are used a day.
- **Many diabetic snack foods have more fat than their regular counterpart**, so the overweight diabetic should avoid such products, for example diabetic chocolates or biscuits.
- **The overweight diabetic should also bear in mind that many diabetic products such as jam or sweets may be blood sugar friendly** (don't cause rapid increases), but may be just as high in Calories as their non-diabetic counterparts.
- **Nutritive sweeteners such as fructose, maltose and sorbitol are as high in energy** as sucrose, can have a laxative effect and can contribute to raised blood sugar levels.
- **Late-night snacks, for example 1 tsp (5 ml) of malted milk powder mixed in 1 glass of skimmed milk or 1 Tbsp (15 ml) of oat bran mixed in a yoghurt, are often important for many diabetics to prevent an overnight drop in blood sugars.**

THE FOLLOWING DIABETIC INDIVIDUALS MAY NEED TO MAKE A CONCERTED EFFORT TO EAT 5–6 SNACKS A DAY

- Those **using insulin**
- **Children and adolescents**
- **Pregnant and breastfeeding women**
- Those who are very **physically active**
- Those trying to **lose weight**

HEALTHY SNACKS INCLUDE:

- **Fruit**, especially citrus or deciduous fruits
- Vegetable **crudités** with low-fat dips (see recipes, pages 106–109) or low-fat or fat-free cottage cheese
- Wholemeal **cereals** with skimmed milk or low-fat yoghurt
- Wholemeal **crispbreads** and bread with low-fat toppings (for the weight conscious diabetic see pages 32–34 for ideas) – avoid jam, honey and other sweet toppings unless they are part of a meal and are used in small amounts.
- Fat-free **yoghurt** or skimmed milk – add 1 Tbsp (15 ml) of oat bran for extra sustenance
- Diabetic **jelly** or fruit with low-fat custard (make instant custard using skimmed milk and sweetener)

- **Tofu** on seedloaf with pickles
- **Three-bean salad**
- **Cold potato salad** made with unpeeled potatoes and a dressing of reduced-calorie mayonnaise and yoghurt
- **Instant porridge** made with skimmed milk
- **Soya milk** and skimmed milk
- **Baked beans** on toast
- **Pasta with pesto sauce, tuna or diced chicken breast**
- Fat-free fruit-flavoured **yoghurt** and fruit salad
- Citrus or deciduous **fruits**
- Bran **muffin** with low-fat or skimmed cottage cheese

It would be best to see a professional dietician or diabetes nurse to work out a snacking plan for you, especially if you fall into one of the above mentioned categories.

GOOD SNACKS FOR THE DIABETIC WHO IS FEELING SICK AND HAS NO APPETITE

- **Milky drinks**, sweetened artificially, such as instant malted milk – use only 1–2 tsp (5–10 ml)
- **Yoghurt**
- Thick **vegetable soup** made with legumes, barley or starchy vegetables, for example minestrone, butternut or pea soup
- Wholemeal **digestive biscuits**

GOOD SNACKS FOR THE DIABETIC WHO EXPERIENCES A DROP IN BLOOD SUGARS

- **3 glucose sweets**
- Half a glass of **Lucozade** or Energade or sweetened cold drink like Coke
- 2 tsp (10 ml) **sugar** dissolved in half a glass of water

The above should be shortly followed by a low GI snack to prevent a rapid increase in blood sugar followed by a rapid drop, such as:

- A wholemeal **sandwich** with a little protein
- Deciduous or citrus **fruit**
- **Baked beans** on toast
- **See low GI foods** on page 19 for more ideas

INSULIN RESISTANCE

Insulin resistance could be preventing you from losing weight.
Clever snacking can help with this.

WHAT IS INSULIN RESISTANCE?

Insulin helps to move glucose from the blood to the body cells where it is used for energy. If you are insulin resistant, the normal amount of insulin produced by the pancreas is not enough for the complete removal of sugar from the blood, and the body produces more insulin in an effort to keep the blood sugar levels normal. As a result, you will often end up with high levels of insulin in your blood. Insulin also encourages fat storage and having too much insulin in your blood will have a negative effect on your weight. Unfortunately, there's a limited amount of insulin in the pancreas, and once depleted, the risk of developing diabetes is almost certain. Insulin resistance is grouped with a number of diseases such as cardiovascular disease, gout, high blood pressure, high cholesterol and diabetes and together they are called syndrome X.

WHAT ARE THE SYMPTOMS?

- **Rapid weight gain and slow weight loss**
- **Unexplained weight loss** with excessive urination and thirst.
- **Fatigue** (especially in the afternoon)
- **Weakness**
- **Irritability and mood swings**
- **Sugar cravings and stimulant cravings,** for example chocolate, coffee and cigarettes

WHAT ARE THE CAUSES?

Obesity (especially where fat is stored in the abdominal area) is still thought to be the number one cause of insulin resistance.

HOW IS IT TESTED?

A fasting glucose and insulin blood sample is required to test for insulin resistance. Further tests may include a glucose tolerance test and glycosylated haemoglobin test. A normal blood glucose level is not uncommon in insulin-resistant people – it does not always have to be high.

HOW CAN YOU PREVENT IT OR IMPROVE THE SYMPTOMS?

Weight loss can usually reverse most of the symptoms and improve your disease profile, but this is often easier said than done.

- **Eat smaller meals** or snacks throughout the day rather than big meals – 5–6 snacky meals are ideal. This will help to control your mood, energy levels and appetite and will prevent high insulin levels.
- **Using the Glycaemic Index** (GI), you need to concentrate on low GI foods such as wholemeal products, beans, oats, fruit and vegetables to ensure a slow release of glucose into the bloodstream, thereby needing only minimal amounts of insulin to be released.
- **Reduce or avoid stimulant intake** such as coffee, tea, alcohol, cigarettes and chocolate.
- **Try to include low-fat protein sources such as tofu, fat-free cottage cheese and fish** with each meal as they can help keep the blood sugars normal.
- **Try to include fatty fish such as mackerel, salmon and tuna** in your diet at least twice a week.
- **Use small amounts of good fats such as avocado, olive oil and nuts** (spread throughout the day), as they don't evoke an insulin response and provide a feeling of fullness after a meal.
- **Try to watch your carbohydrate intake** – consult your dietician for how much you should take in daily. It may need to be reduced more than usual if weight loss is slow.
- **Exercise is essential** to help the glucose and insulin move into the cells, and to help with weight reduction.
- **Smoking can definitely aggravate the situation** – consider reducing the amount you smoke daily or, even better, quit.

Not everyone who battles to lose weight is insulin resistant, but at least we are now more aware as to what it is, and that it could possibly be a reason for slow weight loss. If you think that you could possibly be insulin resistant, contact your dietician who will advise you on further treatment and management.

SNACKING FOR A HEALTHY HEART

FOR THOSE WITH HIGH CHOLESTEROL OR AT RISK OF HEART DISEASE

- 2–4 tsp (10–20 ml) daily unsaturated-fat **margarine** on wholemeal toast or on a baked potato
- 1 Tbsp (15 ml) of **oat bran** in a fat-free yoghurt
- Oat bran **porridge**
- **Olives**
- **Avocado** (have it on crispbreads, on toast or in salads – use vinegar, lemon juice and pepper instead of salt)
- **Nuts and seeds**
- **Peanut butter**
- **Salad** with olives and avocado and with an olive oil-based French dressing
- **Smoked salmon or tuna salad**
- **Pilchards** or sardines on toast
- **Citrus fruits**
- **1–2 glasses red wine** (for those who do not drink alcohol, this is not necessary)
- **Baked beans** on wholemeal toast
- **Sushi**
- **Eat snacks with a low GI** (see page 19)

SNACKING FOR A HEALTHY GUT

- **Probiotics, when they are ingested, are viable micro-organisms that have a beneficial effect in the prevention and treatment of specific pathologic conditions.** They are found in most yoghurts, buttermilk, sour milk, cheese, brewer's yeast and other over-the-counter bacterial preparations.
- **Probiotics can be used to treat gut bacterial infections that have become resistant to antibiotics.** They have also been shown to help with vaginal infections.
- **They can also help with infectious diarrhoea** such as traveller's diarrhoea or rotavirus, irritable bowel, colon cancer, lactose intolerance, HIV diarrhoea and diarrhoea associated with antibiotic use. In the case of traveller's diarrhoea, which occurs in 50% of people, some results of studies have shown that taking either *Lactobacillus, Bifidobacterium* or *Streptococcus* for a week before travelling as well as during travelling, can help reduce the incidence of this rather inconvenient condition.

CONSTIPATION

- **Wholemeal bread** or seedloaf with marmalade
- **Hot liquids** (coffee seems to work well for many people)
- **Water** – with snacks over the whole day
- **More water** (eight glasses a day)
- **Corn on the cob**
- **Muesli** or muesli bar
- Digestive **bran**
- High-fibre breakfast **cereals**
- Dried **fruit**
- **Fruit** with edible skin
- Stewed **prunes**

DIARRHOEA

- Oat **bran**
- **Peeled, seedless fruit**
- **Toast with yeast or meat extract (Marmite or Bovril)**
- **Plenty of fluids with food** – the food helps absorb the fluid
- **Rehydration sachets or make your own rehydration drink** (1 tsp/5 ml salt, 8 tsp/40 ml sugar, 4 cups/1 litre cold water)
- **Avoid dairy** products

INDIGESTION OR HIATUS HERNIA

- **Avoid smoking, caffeine, alcohol, peppermints, fluids with meals or lying down after eating**
- **Eat low-fat snacks** as high-fat foods will linger in your stomach and aggravate indigestion
- **Eat 6 small meals a day** as eating a large meal will increase the pressure in your stomach
- **Eat slowly and chew food** thoroughly
- **Have small amounts of protein** with each meal or snack to act as a buffer against stomach acid

IRRITABLE BOWEL OR SPASTIC COLON

- **Irritable bowel is often a result of stress** – try to reduce stress levels
- **Oats, oat bran and whole grain cereals are good breakfast cereals** – avoid cereals with nuts, seeds and dried fruit
- **Avoid gassy vegetables** such as cauliflower, cabbage, sprouts, onions, etc.
- **Peel all fruit and vegetables**

SNACKING FOR CANCER PREVENTION

Being overweight has been linked to cancer of the breast, endometrium, prostate, colon and rectum, so those at risk of developing cancer should try to lose weight. Also, excessive intake of alcohol and cigarettes as well as preserved and smoked foods should be curtailed. Fresh fruits and vegetables are generally high in antioxidants, which help to 'mop up' any damaging molecules in the body that are derived from pollution, stress, smoking, unhealthy foods, etc.

- **Tomato juice** (tomatoes contain lycopene, which helps protect against prostate cancer specifically)
- **Tomato salad**
- **Tomato and Basil soup** (see recipe, page 102)
- **Soya milk** – use with malted milk powder or in breakfast cereal
- **Tofu** – in salads, in soups and sauces, on baked potatoes
- **Fresh fruit and vegetables**

- **More fresh fruit and vegetables**
- **Crudités** and low-fat dips (see recipes, pages 106–109)
- **Smoothies** (see recipes, pages 120–123) – use soya milk or tofu
- **Garlic bread** (garlic is an antioxidant) (see recipes, page 112)
- **Coleslaw** with a low-fat yoghurt dressing
- **Alcohol-free fruit cocktails**
- **Legumes**, such as baked beans or lentil dip (see recipe, page 108), or thick soup made with lentils and legumes
- **Vitamin C sweets**
- **Nuts and seeds**
- **Oily fish** (pilchards, sardines, tuna, etc.)

SNACKING FOR PREGNANCY AND BREASTFEEDING

To keep the blood sugar levels constant during pregnancy and while nursing, and to prevent constipation common to most pregnant women, snack on the following:

- Bran **muffins** with a thin spreading of honey or jam
- Air-popped **popcorn**
- Fresh **fruit salad**
- **Wholemeal low-fat crispbreads** with a low-fat spread such as yeast or meat extract (Marmite or Bovril), jam, fish paste or low fat cottage or soft cheese
- **Pretzels**
- **Hot cross bun**
- **Wholemeal rusk**
- **A slice of rye bread** with ¼ avocado or low-fat cheese spread
- **Corn cakes** with fresh salsa
- **A bowl of low-fat muesli** and skimmed milk or low fat yoghurt
- **Dried fruit and seed mix** – only a handful at a time!
- **A bowl of fresh steamed vegetables** or crudités with your favourite low-fat dip (see recipes, pages 106–109)

HIGH-CALCIUM SNACKS

- **A glass of hot or cold low-fat or skimmed milk**
- **A mug of instant hot malted milk** with skimmed milk
- **A bowl of low-fat frozen yoghurt or ice-cream**
- **Low-fat yoghurt and fresh fruit smoothie** – try strawberries and/or banana, plain yoghurt and honey
- **Canned sardines** (including the soft bones; they contain calcium) or pilchards with reduced calorie mayonnaise on a slice of toast
- **Tofu** on crispbreads or in a salad
- **Low-fat custard** with canned fruit or jelly
- **Cheddar cheese or a low-fat cheese spread** toasted sandwich
- Skimmed **milkshake**

ANTI-MORNING SICKNESS SNACKS

- **Drink fluid between meals**, not with meals
- **A slice of toast** spread with yeast extract (Marmite) first thing in the morning, before you even leave your bed
- **3 ginger biscuits**
- A **dry rusk**
- **Salty savoury biscuits**

ANTI-HEARTBURN SNACKS

- **Caffeine-free beverages,** e.g. herbal teas (excluding peppermint)
- **Avoid fatty foods,** chocolate, alcohol, peppermints, smoking, citrus juices and tomatoes
- **Drink fluids between meals**
- See also pages 83–84 for **snacks to prevent indigestion and constipation**

LIQUID SNACK FOR THE THIRSTY, BREASTFEEDING MOTHER

Add 1 sachet of a rehydration powder, a mineral supplement and an effervescent multivitamin-mix to 1 litre of water and store in the refrigerator.

SNACKS FOR CHILDREN

GENERAL TIPS

- **Try not to reward, comfort or punish your children with food.**
- **If your child is losing or gaining weight, try not to acknowledge it in an obvious way.** Try to make them feel that you love them and are proud of them no matter how much they weigh.
- **Don't keep junk food at home,** but allow your children to eat junk food (if they want to) out of the home, e.g. when eating out or once a week at the tuck shop.
- **Never say food is fattening or tell your children that they are overweight.** If you wish to tell your overweight child not to eat certain fattening foods, give reasons such as 'its bad for your health, teeth, energy levels', etc.
- **Never talk about your weight or diet problems with your child** – you are their role model so try to achieve healthy eating and weight habits for their sake, if possible.
- **If you are worried that your child is overweight, try changing their diet without them knowing about it.** For example, use less oil when cooking and use low-fat products where possible.
- **If you suspect that your child is overeating for rebellious or attention-seeking reasons, let them see a registered dietician on their own.** Let the dietician be the nagger, not you.
- **Remember that children's bodies often store fat (puppy fat) in preparation for a growth spurt,** so don't panic if your child seems to be suddenly gaining small amounts of weight.
- **As a rule, children below 12 years of age should grow into their weight rather than try to lose weight.** In other words, they should grow taller without gaining much weight.

SNACKS FOR THE OVERWEIGHT CHILD

There is no need to deprive an overweight child of food. Their meals or snacks should still be primarily nutritious, just lower in Calorie density and fat.

FRUIT

- Fresh fruit – 1–3 a day
- Try to limit fruit juice to 250 ml a day, and dilute it with water
- Fruit smoothie: Blend fruit such as bananas or strawberries with fat-free yoghurt or fruit juice
- Fruit dessert: 1 cup (250 ml) canned fruit in natural juice with ½ cup (125 ml) low-fat custard or evaporated milk
- Fruit sosatie: Frozen fruit pieces on a kebab stick
- Freeze Calorie-free cold drink into ice suckers (limit to 1 a day as they will be high in artificial flavourings and colourings). A healthier alternative: freeze fruit juice or chunks of fruit.

MILK

- Cold or hot instant malted milk made with skimmed milk – use 2 tsp (10 ml) per cup (250 ml)
- Fat-free plain or fruit yoghurt
- A scoop of low-fat ice-cream or sorbet in a cone

VEGETABLES

- Raw chopped or sliced carrots, cherry tomatoes, cucumber and mushrooms with fat-free cottage cheese and chutney or low-fat dip (see recipes, pages 106–109)
- Home-made low-fat vegetable soups or instant soups

BREAD

Use wholemeal bread with the following fillings (low-fat or no spread) for in-between meal snacks:

- Yeast or meat extract spread (Marmite or Bovril)
- Jam or honey
- Low-fat cheese spread or wedges
- Fat-free cottage cheese
- Low-fat peanut butter

LOW-FAT, NUTRITIOUS LUNCHBOX IDEAS
FOR OVERWEIGHT CHILDREN

- Sandwiches or crispbreads are always a good option. Try not to use margarine or butter, or use a low-fat spread instead. Easy, low-fat fillings include:
  - Yeast or meat extract spreads (Marmite or Bovril) or fish paste
  - Unprocessed cold meats
  - Low-fat cheese spread or wedges
  - Tuna or white meat chicken with reduced-calorie mayonnaise
  - Jam or honey
  - Low fat soft cheese or fat-free cottage cheese or fromage frais
  - Peanut butter, once or twice a week
  - Add plenty of salad ingredients to make the sandwiches more filling
- **MUFFINS OR CRUMPETS**: make or buy low-fat versions and use jam, honey or cheese spread as fillers
- **BRUMPETS** are an easy alternative. Hot cross buns are also low in fat.
- **FRUIT**: provide a variety, whole or sliced, fresh or dried (in moderation), fruit salad or good quality fruit bars
- **VEGETABLES**: chopped or sliced raw carrots, cherry tomatoes, cucumber and mushrooms with low fat cottage cheese and chutney or low-fat dip
- **YOGHURT**: low fat fruit or plain is best. A canned milkshake can be given occasionally.
- **TREATS**:
  - Air-popped popcorn
  - Low-fat muesli or cereal bar
  - A tube of wine gums
  - A few boiled sweets
  - Marshmallows
  - Small packet of plain pretzels
  - Small packet of low fat crisps
  - Small packet unsalted peanuts and raisins
  - A few low fat plain biscuits or gingernuts
- **IN WINTER**: A flask of instant soup or home-made soup is filling and warming.

SNACKS FOR THE PICKY EATER
These children are usually underweight, and it is easy to add
Calories to their diet by using energy dense snacks.

INGREDIENTS TO BULK UP NORMAL SNACK FOODS
- Peanut butter – use on sandwiches or in smoothies
- Milk powder (must be real dairy, not a milk powder blend) or evaporated milk – add to a glass of milk, over a bowl of cereal, or in a yoghurt
- Soft low-fat spreads – spread on crispbreads and bread before the filling, over vegetables, or in cooked porridge

FRUIT
- Dried fruit snacks – fruit rolls, squares or pieces
- Raisins – on their own, over cereal
- Canned fruit in syrup with ice-cream or custard
- Fresh fruit juices

DAIRY
- Drinking yoghurts
- Smoothies using low-fat yoghurt and flavour with peanut butter or fruit juice/fresh fruit or malted milk powder
- Frozen yoghurt
- Cheese slices or wedges
- Low-fat condensed milk

VEGETABLES
- Thick vegetable soups, such as butternut or pea and ham, with croutons or toast on top

QUICK SNACKS/LUNCHES
- Nuts and seeds – in packets or in the form of a snack bar
- Energy bars, preferably cereal-based
- Oat, yoghurt-coated or choc-chip crunchies
- Two-minute kiddies noodles with frankfurters and cheese
- Canned spaghetti and meat balls
- Toasted sandwiches with high-fat options, e.g. cheese or egg

EATING PLANS EATING PLANS EATING PLANS EATING PLANS EATING

CONVENIENCE SNACKS FOR KIDS IN THE CAR OR ON THE RUN

- **Snack bars** such as breakfast bars, fruit bars, peanut or seed bars, yoghurt bars
- Boxed or canned fresh **fruit juices**
- Individually packed **crispbreads** with cheese wedges
- **Nuts and raisins packs**
- **Small packets of low fat crisps**
- Fresh **fruit**
- Drinking **yoghurt** or milkshakes
- Tubes of **wine gums** or small packets of jelly sweets
- Small packets of **pretzels**
- Packet of **dried fruit** or hot cross buns

PARTY IDEAS FOR KIDS

These snacks are not necessarily low in fat, but they are healthier, more filling and contain less preservatives.

- **Mini pizzas and mini hotdogs**: make your own or buy
- **Popcorn balls**: mix freshly popped popcorn with coloured syrup or honey, form into balls and place on a stick or straw
- **Toffee apples**: keep them busy for longer
- **Orange jelly slices**: set jelly in halved oranges with the flesh scooped out. Once set, cut in half to make quarters.
- **Sandwich shapes**: use yeast extract (Marmite) and cheese to make sandwiches, and then cut into shapes with a biscuit cutter
- **Pretzels and baked corn chips**
- **Punch**: use 100% fruit juice and soda or sparkling water to add a fizz. Freeze extra juice into shaped ice cubes and float them in the punch with freshly chopped fruit.
- **Dried fruit and nut mix**, or peanuts and raisins
- **Fresh fruit skewers**: use chopped seasonal fruit and thin straws or blunt wooden skewers. Serve with a fat-free yoghurt dip.
- **Fruit ices**: use fresh fruit juice to make ice lollies
- **Crudités**: arrange cherry tomatoes, mushrooms, baby corn, cucumber and carrot sticks around a low-fat dip
- **Low-fat sweet faces**: use icing and liquorice to decorate low-fat sweet biscuits to make faces

- **Boudoir/finger biscuit racing cars**: use icing and small sugar-coated jelly sweets for wheels and a jelly baby for the racer
- **Mini chocolate bars**
- **Marshmallow treats**: buy or make your own with puffed rice breakfast cereal and melted marshmallows
- **The cake**: substitute the butter icing with icing made with icing sugar and water to make it less rich

SNACKS FOR TEENAGERS

- **Teenagers are growing so they need extra energy and protein as well as vitamins and minerals.** It is normal for teenagers to be permanently hungry, so make sure they fill up on sandwiches, crispbreads, low-fat muffins, fruit, etc. If weight is an issue, don't limit the bread and fruit too much – rather make sure the sandwich toppings are low fat (see pages 32–34 for ideas).
- **One way to help control or manage a teenager's appetite is to make sure that they eat 6 meals a day** (even if they need to watch their weight).
- **Teenagers should try to eat healthily and low fat as much as possible during the week**, then they can relax at the weekend. For those who are overweight, it might be a good idea to limit the high-fat foods on the weekend as well to about 1–3 treats. It is much easier if unhealthy foods are not available at home during the week.
- **Limit fruit juice intake** – it is quite useful to keep a large jugful of diluted fruit juice (one-third juice to two-thirds water) in the fridge. Avoid keeping carbonated cold drinks at home and limit intake of sweetened cordials. Encourage lots of water drinking.
- **Hamburgers** (preferably flame-grilled chicken burgers) with no sauce or mayonnaise are not such an unhealthy option as long as the chips and sauces are avoided. Use mustard, chutney or tomato sauce with the burger and serve a small coleslaw on the side. If they are still hungry, they can have two hamburgers or just an extra roll.
- **Low-fat sausage rolls** can be made using chicken or turkey sausage or they can eat hot dogs made with reduced-fat frankfurters or pork sausages. Avoid pies and samosas.

- **Pizzas** – opt for vegetable toppings such as spinach, sun-dried tomatoes, asparagus, mushrooms, aubergines, etc. Ask for half the usual amount of cheese or, for the really Calorie conscious, replace the mozzarella with a little strongly flavoured cheese, such as feta, so less will be needed. Have ham, seafood or chicken for meat toppings and avoid bacon, pancetta, sausage, salami and mince.

- **Smoothies** can be made at home or ordered out. They are a great way to take in fruit and dairy, especially when in a hurry. The weight conscious should choose smoothies made only with fresh fruit or those blended with low-fat or fat-free yoghurt or fromage frais. Avoid smoothies that have ice-cream or non-dairy creamers added.

- **Health bars can be misleading** – many so-called health bars have more fat than regular chocolates. Choose low-fat health bars. If they feel like a chocolate, encourage then to have a wafer-based chocolate or muesli bar because there is is less chocolate and therefore less fat.

- **Most sweets, such as jelly babies, boiled sweets, wine gums, etc., are fat free, but they add extra Calories** so they should just have a few if watching their weight.

- **Eat low-fat ice-creams** or eat fruity ice lollies.

- **Chips or crisps are generally unhealthy.** Look out for baked or low-fat varieties and allow only a small packet occasionally. Pretzels and popcorn are a healthier option but they are not necessarily lower in fat.

Most of these recipes are low in fat and therefore are also low in cholesterol. Apart from some of the smoothies, they are suitable for diabetics, but many of the recipes are not suitable for weight gain.

Try using whole flour or oats, or even better oat bran, in place of regular flour in your recipes.

RECIPES

TIPS FOR LOW-FAT SHOPPING

- **There is nearly always a low- or lower-fat option available.** Initially you will need to spend some time trying to identify these products, but once you know where they are and what they look like, it will become easier.

- **Plan ahead what you are going to eat for the week** so that you can buy the necessary ingredients. It is very frustrating trying to cook something new without the correct ingredients.

- **Write out a shopping list and stick to it.**

- **Never go shopping when you are hungry.**

- **Keep an eye out for NEW, lower-fat options** – food manufacturers are realizing the need for low-fat products.

- **Reduced fat does not mean low fat.** A reduced-fat product only has to have a given percentage less fat and can therefore still be a high-fat product (e.g. reduced-fat cheese). See also page 16.

- **Low fat does not mean fat free.** See also page 16.

- **A low GI food does not mean that it is a healthy or diet food item** – many low GI foods are high in fat, cholesterol or Calories.

- **Sucrose-free diabetic chocolate has a higher fat content than most regular chocolates.** Be wary of so-called diabetic products.

- **Look at the fat content per portion size** rather than per 100 g. A product such as breadcrumbs will have a high fat content per 100 g, but the fat content per portion size is likely to be negligible.

- **Become a sceptic.** Look-out for products that make statements that could be misinterpreted. For example, a sweet-tasting product that states 'no sugar added' may already contain sugar in its natural form, e.g. fruit juice already contains fructose (fructose has the same Calories as sucrose).

- Read food labels carefully and **think about what a label is NOT saying,** i.e. fat free does not mean sugar free and the product may still be high in Calories. Cholesterol free does not mean fat free. A bottle of vegetable oil may be cholesterol free but it is still a 100% fat product and the Calorie content will be just as high.

- **Read the front of the packaging briefly and the back slowly and carefully.** The most important information for you may be in small print, and might even be hidden in the folds of the wrapping.

- **Ingredients are listed in order of weight,** i.e. largest (by weight) ingredient first on the list and the smallest ingredient last. Therefore, if the food you are trying to avoid is in the top five ingredients, you should probably not buy that product.

- **If in doubt, contact the manufacturer.** Contact details should always be on the back of products.

- **Look-out for disguises.** Learn aliases: fat can be called hydrogenated fat, shortening or lard. Sugar can be called sucrose, glucose, fructose, maltose, cane sugar, corn syrup or sorbitol.

- **Be ready for chemical warfare.** Look for products that are free of chemicals. Many manufacturers are trying to make products without adding flavourings, colourings or preservatives.

- **Be prepared to pay the price.** A standard product that is naturally high in an ingredient may be overcompensated with another ingredient to make up for the loss of that particular main ingredient when the product is altered. For example, sugar is a big part of chocolate and therefore diabetic chocolate usually has more fat than regular chocolate to make up for the decrease in sugar. These products are usually more expensive too.

- **You still need to live**. Don't get too caught up in label reading. Sometimes you simply need to enjoy a product for its taste, ability to fill a hole or for its convenience.

SHOPPING LIST FOR LOW-FAT SNACKS/FOODS THAT SHOULD ALWAYS BE AVAILABLE

- Low-fat or fat-free **yoghurt**
- **Skimmed milk** – keep a few cartons of long-life skimmed milk at home and at work for emergencies
- Fat-free **cottage cheese or fromage frais**
- Fresh **fruit**
- **Dried fruit or fruit bars**
- **Fresh vegetable and salad ingredients**
- Oil-free **salad dressing** and/or reduced calorie mayonnaise
- Low-fat **savoury biscuits, or crispbreads**
- Sliced **bread** – keep a loaf in the freezer for emergencies
- Low-fat breakfast **cereal**
- Two-minute low-fat **instant noodles**
- Reduced-fat **cheese wedges**
- Canned **tuna** in brine
- **Fish paste**
- **Low-fat snack bars**
- **Low-fat sweet biscuits**
- **Low-fat ready meals** – keep a few packs in the freezer for those days when you don't feel like cooking
- **Low-fat hot chocolate powder**

TIPS FOR LOW-FAT COOKING

- **Make the same recipes you have always made, just leave out the fat.** You don't have to change your normal way of cooking; the changes you make must be permanent so make sure that they're easy to sustain.
- **Keep a few low-fat, instant meals** on standby for when you don't feel like cooking and the rest of the family are ordering take-aways.
- **Keep the rest of the family happy** – put full-fat salad dressings, sauces or butter on the table for them to help themselves. Hopefully they'll follow your lead and choose the healthier option.
- **Don't tell your family that the lasagne or casserole is low fat.** If you do tell them they will all complain that they can't eat diet food. If you don't tell them, they won't know any different.

LOW-FAT COOKING EQUIPMENT

- **Wok** – ideal for low-fat stir-fries
- **Non-stick pans and baking trays** – ideal for preparing low-fat meals as you won't need to use oil or butter for greasing
- **Roasting pan with built-in rack** – the fat drips into the pan below
- **Steamer** – bamboo or steel
- **Microwave** – vital for heating low-fat freezer meals, quick-baked potatoes, popcorn, etc.
- **Sandwich toaster** – they are usually non-stick so you won't need to use any fat on your toasted sandwiches
- **Blender** (the hand-held ones are very convenient) – vital for smoothies or making thick, creamy vegetable soups
- **A very sharp knife or kitchen scissors** – for trimming excess fat
- **A spray bottle** (multi-use sprayer) for spraying olive oil – if you mix water with the olive oil, the oil mist comes out very fine

MUST-HAVE FOOD ITEMS FOR LOW-FAT COOKING

- Olive oil spray or non-stick spray for frying
- Soy sauce, sherry, wine, stock, balsamic vinegar or fruit juice for stir-frying or browning onions, meat or chicken. Add water, wine, fruit or vegetable juices if more liquid is needed.
- Reduced-fat coconut milk
- Low-fat evaporated milk, skimmed milk, fat-free plain yoghurt

98

or buttermilk instead of cream

- Strong-flavoured cheese, such as mature Cheddar or Parmesan
- MSG-free vegetable stock powder
- Flour and gravy browing powder for thickening
- Low-fat condiments (see page 35)

LOW-FAT REPLACEMENTS FOR CHEESE

- Use Parmesan or extra mature Cheddar cheese; you will have to add much less to get the same flavour
- Use low-fat cheese spread or wedges on pizzas or sandwiches
- Ricotta, fat-free fromage frais or cottage cheese

LOW-FAT PASTRY

- Phyllo pastry
- For tarts/quiches: mashed potato or rice mixed with egg white. Bake the base for 10 minutes in a moderate oven before filling.

LOW-FAT SALAD DRESSINGS

- Balsamic or fruit-flavoured vinegar
- Lemon juice and herbs
- Tomato or vegetable juice, vinegar, herbs and sugar
- Mustard, honey and lemon juice
- A variety of reduced-calorie salad dressings are commercially available

LOW-FAT REPLACEMENTS FOR CREAMY SAUCES

- Buttermilk or fat-free yoghurt (they will curdle if boiled)
- Low-fat evaporated milk
- Fat-free white sauce (see recipe, page 107)
- Reduced-fat coconut milk

LOW-FAT DESSERTS AND BAKING

- For desserts like cheesecake, use fat-free cottage cheese, fromage frais or low-fat soft cheese instead of regular cream cheese
- Use buttermilk or fat-free plain yoghurt instead of fresh cream
- Use fruit purée, juice or buttermilk to reduce the fat content
- Use low-fat ice-cream instead of regular ice-cream

SKINNY SOUPS

Make double pots of soup and freeze the leftovers in small containers for when you need it. If you don't like using stock cubes, make fresh stock or just use water and add extra seasoning.

CARROT AND CORIANDER SOUP

serves 4–6

5 ml (1 tsp) crushed **garlic**
1 **onion**, chopped
5 ml (1 tsp) crushed **ginger**, or about 4 cm fresh
root ginger, peeled and grated
2 **stock cubes** dissolved in 1 litre (4 cups) boiling water
1 kg **carrots**, topped, tailed and sliced
125 ml (½ cup) chopped fresh **coriander** leaves

Brown the **garlic**, **onion** and **ginger** in a little **stock**
for 6–8 minutes. Add the **carrots** and remaining **stock**
and cook until the carrots are tender. Add the **coriander**
about 5 minutes before the end of cooking time.
Remove from heat and liquidize until smooth.
Garnish with fresh **coriander** leaves. Serve hot
or cold with fresh, crusty **bread**.

1 serving (1 cup) = 1 portion carbohydrate

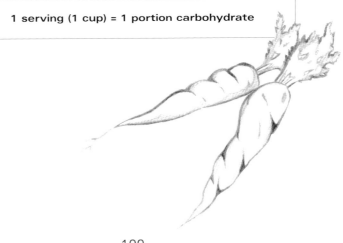

100

RICH BABY COURGETTE AND CHEESE SOUP

serves 6

1 **onion**, roughly chopped

5 ml (1 tsp) crushed **garlic**

2 **chicken stock cubes** dissolved in

2 litres (8 cups) boiling **water**

900 g **courgettes**,

roughly chopped

1 unpeeled **potato**, diced

40 g **blue cheese** or feta

750 ml (3 cups) shredded **spinach**

125 ml (½ cup) low-fat evaporated **milk** or skimmed milk

(optional)

salt and freshly ground black **pepper** to taste

Cook the **onion** and **garlic** in a little of the **stock** until soft, then add the **courgettes** and **potatoes**. Add the rest of the **stock** and crumbled **cheese** and allow to simmer until the **potato** and **courgettes** are soft. Add the **spinach** towards end of the cooking time. Leave to cool then blend for about 1 minute (it should still be quite chunky). Return to heat and add the evaporated or skimmed **milk** (if using) and seasoning.

---

1 serving = contribution to Calorie intake is negligible

Serve hot with crispy **Italian rolls**.

NOTE: This soup is low in Calories and is therefore unsuitable for those trying to gain weight or those who need to raise the energy content of their diet.

CHILLED SUMMER SOUP

serves 2-3

300 ml (1¼ cups) **tomato juice**
300 ml (1¼ cups) fat-free plain **yoghurt**
grated rind and juice of ½ **orange**
2.5 cm thick slice of **cucumber**, finely chopped
1 **red or yellow pepper**, seeded and chopped
salt and freshly ground black **pepper** to taste

Whisk together **tomato juice** and **yoghurt**. Add remaining
ingredients and liquidize. Check seasoning and chill.
Serve with crusty **baguettes** or wholemeal **rolls**.

1 serving = contribution to Calorie intake is negligible

TOMATO AND BASIL SOUP

serves 6

3 x 410 g tins peeled, chopped **tomatoes** or 900 g fresh, ripe
tomatoes (If using fresh tomatoes: place the tomatoes in
boiling water for 1 minute, then peel off the skin.)
65g can **tomato puree**
20 ml (4 tsp) **sugar**
2 **stock cubes** dissolved in 750 ml (3 cups) boiling water
45 ml (3 Tbsp) chopped fresh **basil** leaves

Cook all the ingredients except the **basil** together until the
tomatoes are soft. Cool slightly, then liquidize and serve
garnished with chopped fresh **basil**. If using fresh
tomatoes, you can precook the tomatoes on their own
and then strain them to remove the pulp and seeds.

1 serving = contribution to Calorie intake is negligible

CREAMY MUSHROOM SOUP

serves 4

500 g **mushrooms**, roughly chopped
1 large handful fresh **parsley**, chopped
5 ml (1 tsp) crushed **garlic**
2 **chicken stock** cubes dissolved in
750 ml (3 cups) boiling **water**
2 slices white **bread**, crusts removed
1 ml (¼ tsp) grated **nutmeg**
salt and freshly ground black **pepper** to taste
½ x 410 g can low-fat evaporated **milk** or
125 ml (½ cup) skimmed milk

Fry **mushrooms, parsley** and **garlic** for a few minutes
in a little chicken **stock**. Cover and leave to simmer for
10 minutes, making sure there is just enough liquid.
Crumble **bread** into saucepan and add remaining
stock, nutmeg and **seasoning**. Simmer for another
10 minutes and then liquidize. Add evaporated
milk or skimmed milk, reheat and serve.

---

1 serving = contribution to Calorie intake is negligible

NOTE: This soup is low in Calories
and is therefore unsuitable for
those trying to gain weight.
It is, however, a good
source of calcium.

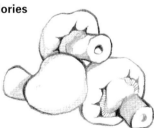

SKINNY SALADS

GREEN SALAD WITH TANGY MANGO AND MINT DRESSING

serves 4–6

shredded **lettuce** leaves

Chinese **cabbage**

spring onions

green pepper, seeded and cut into strips

cucumber slices

1 **mango**, peeled and sliced

flaked **almonds** to garnish

DRESSING

1 red **chilli**, finely chopped

1 ripe **mango**, peeled and pip removed

15 ml (1 Tbsp) fruit **chutney**

175 ml (3/4 cup) low-fat plain **yoghurt**

30 ml (2 Tbsp) low-fat **coconut milk**

30 ml (2 Tbsp) chopped fresh **mint** leaves

Prepare a tossed **salad** and top with **mango** slices.
To make the **dressing**, combine all the ingredients and
blend in a food processor until smooth. Drizzle the
salad with dressing and garnish with the **almonds**.
Serve well chilled, with crusty **bread**.

---

1 serving = contribution to Calorie intake is negligible

CUCUMBER SALAD
serves 4

1 **cucumber** (unpeeled) grated and drained for 30 minutes
80 ml (⅓ cup) reduced-calorie **mayonnaise**
160 ml (⅔ cup) fat-free plain **yoghurt**

Mix all the ingredients together and serve chilled.

---

1 serving = 1 portion fat

FETA AND CORN SALAD
serves 2

1 x 410 g can **corn** kernels, drained
8 x 1.5 cm round of **feta**, cubed
a handful of cherry **tomatoes**

Mix all the ingredients together. Grind over black **pepper**
just before serving with **low-fat dressing** if desired.

---

1 serving = 1 portion carbohydrate and 1 portion protein

SALAD DRESSING
makes about 400 ml

250 ml (1 cup) **vinegar** of your choice
80 ml (⅓ cup) prepared **mustard** of your choice
80 ml (⅓ cup) **honey**

Mix all the ingredients together and drizzle over **salad**.

---

1 serving (1 Tbsp) = free

SKINNY DIPS

SPICY CREAM CHEESE DIP

serves 4–8 and takes 5 minutes to prepare

226 g block low-fat **soft cheese**
1 x 410 g can or jar **Mexican tomato sauce** or
⅓ x 470g jar hot tomato **chutney**
fresh **coriander**

Unwrap **soft cheese** and place in microwaveable serving
dish. Pour over the **tomato sauce** or **chutney** (or make
your own). Heat on high for 1 minute. Garnish with fresh
coriander and serve with low-fat **savoury biscuits**.

> 1 serving (1 heaped Tbsp) dip = 1 portion protein
> 3 cream crackers or 5 water biscuits =
> 1 portion carbohydrate

GUACAMOLE

serves 4–6

1 **avocado**
250 ml (1 cup) fat-free **cottage cheese**
15 ml (1 Tbsp) **lemon juice**
5 ml (1 tsp) snipped **chives**
salt and freshly ground black **pepper** to taste

Mix all the ingredients and serve with **crudités**
or **potato skins** (see recipe, page 113).

> 1 serving = 1 portion fat and 1 portion protein

**NOTE: This dip is a good source of mono-unsaturated
fats**, which have cholesterol-lowering properties.

FAT-FREE HUMMUS

serves 4–6

Traditionally, hummus is made with lots of olive oil, which
is a pity as it is a delicious and nutritious vegetarian
spread or dip. This recipe is not only easy to make, but is
also fat free so enjoy lavish smearings of it on bread,
savoury biscuits and baked potatoes or use as a dip
for crudités.

1 x 425 g can **chickpeas** (liquid included)
juice of 1 **lemon**
2–3 cloves **garlic**
2.5 ml (½ tsp) ground **cumin**
a sprinkling of **cayenne pepper**

Place all the ingredients into a liquidizer
and process to a fine paste.

---

1 serving (3 Tbsp) = 1 portion carbohydrate
and 1 portion protein

FOR THE LAZY CHEF: Buy ready-made reduced-fat
hummus and tzatziki for an occasional treat.

LOW-FAT WHITE SAUCE

Heat **skimmed milk** until just before boiling point. Mix a
little **cornflour** in a small amount of cold **milk**. Add the
cold paste to the hot milk while stirring and bring to the
boil. Keep adding paste and stirring until you reach the
desired consistency, then add **flavouring** such as herbs,
spices or cheese.

SPICY LENTIL DIP
WITH POPPADUMS

serves 8

125 ml (½ cup) each brown and red **lentils**

15 ml (1 Tbsp) **olive oil**

1 **onion**, chopped

7.5 ml (½ Tbsp) crushed **garlic**

5 ml (1 tsp) **turmeric**

5 ml (1 tsp) ground **cumin**

2.5 ml (½ tsp) **chilli powder**

1 handful fresh **coriander** leaves

30 ml (2 Tbsp) **lemon juice**

salt to taste

ready-to-cook **poppadums**

Soak the **lentils** for a few hours (or overnight) in water.
Drain. Cook for 30 minutes and then drain and wash well.
Heat **oil** in large frying pan and sauté **onion** until soft.
Add **garlic** and **spices** and cook for a few minutes.
Blend this mixture with the **lentils, coriander** and
lemon juice. Add **salt**. Refrigerate before serving
with microwaved **poppadums** (microwave on high
for 1 minute on each side).

---

1 serving dip = 1 portion carbohydrate and
1 portion protein
3 poppadums = ½ portion carbohydrate
and 1 portion fat

**NOTE: Lentils (and legumes) are excellent for controlling
blood sugars** and reducing cholesterol levels because
of their high soluble fibre content.

TZATZIKI

serves 4

2 x 175 g fat-free plain **yoghurt**
4 ml (¾ tsp) **garlic paste**
½ **cucumber**, julienned and drained
in a sieve for 30 minutes
1–2 **gherkins**, very finely chopped
a few chopped **mint** leaves or
15 ml (1 Tbsp) **lemon juice** (optional)

Pour the **yoghurt** into a mixing bowl and add **garlic** paste.
Add the **cucumber** and **gherkins** to yoghurt mixture and
pour some gherkin juice in afterwards. Add **mint** and
lemon juice (if using). Stir well and refrigerate. Serve chilled.

> **1 serving = free**

MANGO AND CHILLI DIP

serves 6

250 ml (1 cup) fat-free **cottage cheese**
1 large **mango**, finely chopped
±15 ml (1 Tbsp) **chilli jam** or 1 fresh red **chilli**, chopped
15 ml (1 Tbsp) **apricot jam**
30 ml (2 Tbsp) **lemon juice**
salt and freshly ground black **pepper** to taste

Mix all the ingredients together and serve
with **crudités** or **melba toast**.

> **1 serving = 1 portion protein**

CARBOHYDRATE SNACKS

PHYLLO PASTRY TARTLETS
serves 4

These tarts are much easier to make than you think.

2 sheets **phyllo pastry**
1 **egg white** mixed with 125 ml (½ cup) **skimmed milk**
salt and freshly ground black **pepper** to taste
low-free **soft cheese** mixed with a little
grated extra mature **Cheddar cheese**
1 handful of fresh **basil** leaves
3 small **tomatoes** or 8 cherry tomatoes, sliced

Preheat the oven to 200 °C (400 °F). Brush **phyllo** sheets with **egg white** and **milk** mixture and cut into sixteen 10 cm squares. Place two squares on top of each other and arrange in a patty tin that has been sprayed with cooking spray. Sprinkle with **salt** and **pepper** and spread soft **cheese** mixture over the top. Place a few **basil** leaves on each pastry pile. Arrange sliced **tomatoes** on top and bake for 10–12 minutes until golden. Serve while still warm.

---

3 tarts = 1 portion carbohydrate and 1 portion protein

DECADENT ALTERNATIVE: Top with canned asparagus pieces instead of tomatoes and basil.

SPINACH QUICHE
serves 6

500 ml (2 cups) cooked, shredded **spinach**
2 **egg** yolks and 4 egg whites, beaten
2 slices wholemeal **bread** soaked in
125 ml (½ cup) **skimmed milk**
5 ml (1 tsp) crushed **garlic**
salt and freshly ground black **pepper** to taste
15 ml (1 Tbsp) grated strong-flavoured **cheese**

Preheat oven to 180 °C (350 °F). Mix together all the ingredients, except the **cheese**. Wipe a quiche dish with **olive oil** or use non-stick spray. Press the mixture into the dish and sprinkle with the **cheese**. Bake for 15 minutes, or until **cheese** is melted and golden brown on top.

---

1 serving = 1 portion protein

NOTE: This quiche is an excellent source of vitamins and minerals due to the spinach and wholewheat bread.

POPPADUMS

Place ready-to-cook (spiced or plain) **poppadums** in microwave straight on turntable. Do a few at a time, as they will not cook evenly if placed on top of each other. Microwave on high for 1 minute and then turn over and microwave for a further minute on the other side. Or bake or grill in the oven if you prefer. Serve whole or broken up into quarters with **dips** and **curries**.

**3 poppadums = ½ portion carbohydrate
and 1 portion fat**

NOTE: Poppadums are a great substitute for crisps.

FRENCH GARLIC BREAD
serves 6

1 French **loaf** (or rye bread), sliced and toasted
without margarine or butter
fresh whole **garlic** cloves
fresh ripe **tomatoes**, halved
salt and freshly ground black **pepper** to taste

Rub the **garlic** cloves over the still-hot toasted **French loaf.**
Squeeze the **tomatoes** over the bread. Season and enjoy.

> **3 x 1 cm-slices French loaf or 1 slice rye bread =
> 1 portion carbohydrate**

NOTE: Garlic has excellent health promocang properties
and strengthens the heart and immune system.

CHEESY GARLIC BREAD
serves 6

45 ml (3 Tbsp) low-fat processed **cheese spread**
(preferably cheddar flavour)
10 ml (2 tsp) crushed **garlic**
1 small **French loaf**, sliced not quite all the way
through into uniform slices

Mix the **cheese spread** and **garlic**. Spoon about 5 ml (1 tsp)
of the mixture between each slice of **French loaf**. Wrap
the loaf in foil and bake at 180 °C (350 °F) until the
cheese has melted. Open the foil for the last few
minutes and grill the bread until golden brown on top.
Serve at a barbecue or just as a filling snack or starter.

> **3 x 1 cm-slices French loaf = 1 portion carbohydrate**

POTATO SKINS
serves 4 (makes 8 skins)

4 large baking **potatoes**
chilli powder to taste
10 ml (2 tsp) **paprika**
5 ml (1 tsp) ground **cumin**
2.5 ml (½ tsp) **garlic powder**
2.5 ml (½ tsp) **onion powder**
2.5 ml (½ tsp) dried **oregano**
1 ml (¼ tsp) **salt**
finely grated **Parmesan cheese**
olive oil spray

Scrub the **potatoes**, prick with a fork and then bake
at 200 °C (400 °F) until done (about 1 hour, depending
on size). Mix together all dry ingredients, including
cheese. Cut **potatoes** in half lengthwise and scoop out
the centre (use the pulp to make **mashed potatoes**),
leaving a 3 mm thick shell. Spray the inside of the
skins with **olive oil** spray and then sprinkle evenly with
dry ingredients. Bake at 200 °C (400 °F) for 10 minutes,
or until crispy. Serve hot with **salsa** or leave to cool
before storing in an airtight container.

2 skins = 1 portion carbohydrate

ONE-MINUTE MASH
serves 4

4 large or 8 medium **potatoes**, cooked
(to increase the fibre and nutrient content, do not peel)
200 ml (¾ cup) **skimmed milk, buttermilk or stock**
(it is not necessary to add margarine or butter) OR low-fat
evaporated milk to thin down the mash
(for those who like very creamy mashed potatoes)
salt and freshly ground black **pepper** to taste
snipped **chives**
green, yellow and red peppers or spinach sautéed
in stock to add colour (optional)

Blend all the ingredients together using a hand-blender
to get creamy, lump-free mash in 1 minute.

---

1 cup mash = 2 portions carbohydrate

QUICK ALTERNATIVE: Instant mashed potato – origi-
nal plain or flavoured – just add boiling water. Serve with
grilled low-fat pork sausages for a dieter's version of
Bangers and Mash, or ask your local butcher to make
sausages for you using only lean mince with no added fat.

**NOTE: Potatoes are a good source of energy,
fibre, vitamins and minerals.**

QUICK SCRAMBLED EGG

serves 1

1–2 **eggs**
a dash of **skimmed milk**
salt and freshly ground black **pepper** to taste
a pinch of dried mixed **herbs**

Beat the **eggs and milk** in a coffee mug with a fork.
Add **seasoning** and **herbs**. Microwave on high for
30-second periods, stirring after each 30 seconds,
until cooked. If preferred, cook in a frying pan sprayed
with **olive oil** spray or use a non-stick pan. For interescang
variations, fold snipped **chives**, smoked **salmon, ham**
or grilled lean **bacon** into the cooked **egg** mixture.
Serve on wholemeal **toast** or **seedloaf**, or a toasted
English **muffin**. It's also great with a fresh **bagel**.
Garnish with slices of **tomato**.

---

1 egg = 1 portion protein

**NOTE: If you have high cholesterol, limit your egg intake
to three eggs a week.** Otherwise, four eggs a week is
the general health recommendation. The cholesterol and
fat is in the yolk, so you can have extra egg whites,
which are a good source of protein.

FAT-FREE MICROWAVED POPCORN

I prefer to make my own rather than buy the flavoured microwave popcorn. If you have a popcorn machine, you will not need to use oil. Stove-top preparation requires oil and effort whereas microwave preparation requires neither of these.

Line a large mixing bowl with a paper towel. Throw **popcorn kernels** into the bowl and cover the bowl with a dinner plate. Cook in the microwave for 2–3 minutes on high or listen for when most of the popping stops. Add flavouring straight away otherwise it won't stick to the popcorn. Spraying the popcorn with a fine mist of water, vinegar or lemon juice (or a mixture) also helps.

SUGGESTED FLAVOURINGS

Cheese powder

Celery salt

Herb salt

Chilli powder

Barbecue spice

1½ cups popped popcorn = 1 portion carbohydrate

PANCAKES
makes 8

250 ml (1 cup) **flour** (preferably wholemeal)
1 ml (¼ tsp) **baking powder**
2.5 ml (½ tsp) **salt**
250 ml (1 cup) **skimmed milk**
1 large **egg**, beaten

Mix dry ingredients. Add a little **milk** and stir until smooth. Keep adding **milk** gradually. Add **egg** and beat well. Lightly grease a non-stick frying pan using a little non-stick or **olive oil** spray and pour in a little of the pancake mixture to cover base of pan. Cook until lightly browned on both sides.

SWEET
Serve with **cinnamon sugar** and a wedge of **lemon** or serve with a drizzle of **honey or maple syrup**.

SAVOURY
Serve pancakes with low-fat or fat-free **cottage cheese** or **feta** mixed with cooked **spinach and mushrooms** (stir-fry in a little stock).

---

1 pancake = 1 portion carbohydrate

NOTE: Using wholemeal flour adds vitamins and minerals, as well as fibre.

SKINNY TREATS

RUSKS
makes 25 rusks

45 ml (3 Tbsp) polyunsaturated **margarine**, melted
1 **egg**
250 ml (1 cup) **buttermilk** or low-fat or fat-free plain **yoghurt**
250 ml (1 cup) fat-free **milk**
875 ml (3½ cups) **self-raising flour**
125 ml (½ cup) **sugar**

Beat together **margarine, egg, buttermilk** and **milk**. Stir in **flour** and **sugar** until a soft dough forms. Roll into balls and place close together in a greased baking can. Bake at 180 °C (350 °F) for 30 minutes, or until a knife comes out clean when balls are pierced. Remove from oven and leave to cool slightly. Break into pieces and return to oven for 3–4 hours at 100 °C (200 °F), or until rusks have dried out.

> 1 rusk = 1 portion carbohydrate

DATE AND BRAN MUFFINS
makes 16–18

1 x 250 g block (¾ cup) **dates**, pitted and finely chopped
125 ml (½ cup) **raisins**
250 ml (1 cup) boiling **water**
10 ml (2 tsp) **bicarbonate of soda**
750 ml (3 cups) **wholemeal flour**
60 ml (¼ cup) **soft brown sugar**
1 **egg**, beaten
250 ml (1 cup) **buttermilk**
5 ml (1 tsp) **vanilla extract**

118

Mix the **dates** and **raisins** with boiling **water** and 5 ml (1 tsp) **bicarbonate of soda**. Set aside to soak. Mix the **flour, sugar** and remaining **bicarbonate of soda** in a mixing bowl. Beat together the **egg, buttermilk** and **vanilla extract** and add to the date mixture. Add the liquid mixture to the dry ingredients and mix lightly until a moist dough is formed – don't overmix. Spoon the dough into a greased muffin tray until the cups are each two-thirds full. Bake for 15–20 minutes at 200 °C (400 °F) until well risen. Allow to cool slightly, then turn muffins out onto a rack.

---

1 muffin = 1 portion carbohydrate and 1 portion fruit

FAT-FREE FRUIT CAKE
makes 15 slices

400 g (2½ cups) mixture of **raisins and sultanas**
300 ml (1¼ cups) **soft brown sugar**
625 ml (2½ cups) **plain flour**
1 **egg**, beaten
10 ml (2 tsp) **baking powder**
2.5 ml (½ tsp) each grated **nutmeg** and **mixed spice**
1 ml (¼ tsp) each **ground ginger, cinnamon** and **cloves**

Cover fruit with water (add 90 ml/6 Tbsp **brandy** for the extra touch!) and leave to soak overnight. Mix all the ingredients together including the fruit and soaking liquid to give the mixture a softish consistency. Spoon into a small loaf tin and bake at 160 °C (325 °F) for 1¾–2 hours.

---

1 slice = 1 portion carbohydrate and 1 portion fruit

NOTE: Diabetics should only eat this cake in very small portions, preferably with a meal. Diabetics with uncontrolled blood sugars should avoid this altogether.

SMOOTHIES

Smoothies are ideal for those who struggle
to eat enough fresh fruit and dairy.

DAIRY FREE
Where milk is called for in a recipe, soya milk can be
substituted for those wishing to avoid dairy.

INTERESTING INFORMATION

If using citrus fruit, leave as much as possible of the white pith
when peeling, as it is high in nutrients. When blending apples,
just remove the stem – the core and pips are high in nutrition and
blend well. Drink the smoothie as soon as possible after blending
to ensure optimum nutritional value as well as taste quality.

INTERESTING INFORMATION

DIETER'S FRUITY SMOOTHIE
serves 2

Low in calories, yet high in fibre,
vitamins and minerals.

500 ml (2 cups) fresh/frozen **mixed berries** (use cranberries
if you suffer from urinary tract problems)
250 ml (1 cup) **crushed ice**
125 ml (½ cup) **grapefruit juice** or 15 ml (1 Tbsp) **lemon juice**

Blend all the ingredients together and serve immediately.

1 serving = 1 portion fruit

HIGH-ENERGY SMOOTHIE
(ICED COFFEE OR VANILLA FLAVOUR)
serves 1

This smoothie is high in saturated fats, which are partly responsible for high blood cholesterol. Avoid it if you have high cholesterol, are trying to lose weight, are diabetic or have heart disease. It is, however, ideal for someone trying to gain weight.

10 ml (2 tsp) **instant coffee powder** or 5 ml (1 tsp) **vanilla essence**
60 ml (¼ cup) **boiling water**
125 ml (½ cup) **evaporated milk**
250 ml (1 cup) full-cream **milk**
2 scoops **ice-cream**
10 ml (2 tsp) **sugar**

Add **coffee** to boiling **water** and leave to cool. Blend **coffee** with remaining ingredients and serve immediately.

NOTE: This recipe is for weight gain, therefore portion control is irrelevant. If you are trying to gain weight, have as much as you can comfortably consume.

REFRESHER SMOOTHIE
serves 1

125 ml (½ cup) **apple juice**
1 **Granny Smith apple**, peeled and chopped
125 ml (½ cup) fat-free plain **yoghurt**
125 ml (½ cup) crushed **ice**
a pinch of ground **cinnamon**

Blend ingredients, sprinkle with extra **cinnamon** and serve.

1 serving = 2 portions fruit and 1 portion dairy

HIGH-FIBRE SMOOTHIE

serves 2

This low-fat, dairy free smoothie is perfect for someone
suffering from constipation or not getting enough fibre
(this includes most of us who eat processed, instant
foods). Drink at least two glasses of water with this
smoothie and make sure that you have at least six
glasses of fluid over the whole day in order for this
smoothie to take effect.

10 ml (2 tsp) **bran**
250 ml (1 cup) **pawpaw**, peeled, seeded and chopped
250 ml (1 cup) **orange segments**
1 ripe **banana**
3 soft-cooked or canned and pitted **prunes**
or 125 ml (½ cup) prune juice

Blend all the ingredients together and serve immediately.

1 serving = 2 portions fruit

DIETER'S DECADENT SMOOTHIE

serves 3

250 ml (1 cup) skimmed **milk**
250 ml (1 cup) fat-free plain **yoghurt**
1 scoop low-fat frozen **yoghurt or ice-cream**
1 x 410 g can unsweetened **peaches**, drained
15 ml (1 Tbsp) crystallized **ginger**

Blend all the ingredients together and serve immediately.

1 serving = 1 portion dairy and 1 portion fruit

HIGH-PROTEIN, HIGH-ENERGY, HIGH-CALCIUM, LOW-FAT SMOOTHIE

serves 1

This smoothie is suitable for those trying to gain weight.

250 ml (1 cup) skimmed **milk**
125 ml (½ cup) fat-free plain **yoghurt**
30 ml (2 Tbsp) skimmed **milk powder**
1 ripe **banana**
100 g (½ cup) soft **tofu** (if available)
a pinch each of ground **cinnamon** and **allspice**
15 ml (1 Tbsp) **honey**

Blend all the ingredients together and serve immediately.

NOTE: This recipe is for weight gain, therefore portion control is irrelevant. If you are trying to gain weight, have as much as you can comfortably consume.

IMMUNE BOOSTER

serves 2

250 ml (1 cup) grated **carrots**
250 ml (1 cup) **orange segments**
or freshly squeezed orange juice
250 ml (1 cup) fresh **strawberries**
125 ml (½ cup) **apple juice**
20 ml (4 tsp) freshly **ground seeds or nuts**

Blend all the ingredients together and serve immediately.

1 serving = 1 portion fat and 2 portions fruit

AUSTRALIA

Diabetes Australia
Level 5, 39 London Circuit
Canberra City
ACT 2600
Tel: (02) 6232 3800
www.diabetesaustralia.com.au

Food Standards Australia
Boeing House
55 Blackhall Street
Barton
ACT 2600
Tel: (02) 6271 2222
Fax: (02) 6271 2278
www.anzfa.gov.au

National Heart Foundation of Australia
Cnr Denison St & Geils Court
Deakin
ACT 2600
Tel: (1300) 36 27 87
www.heartfoundation.com.au

NEW ZEALAND

Diabetes New Zealand
www.diabetes.org.nz

Food Standards New Zealand
Level 4, 108 The Terrace
Wellington
Tel: (04) 473 9942
Fax: (04) 473 9855
www.anzfa.gov.au

The Heart Foundation, New Zealand
www.nhf.org.nz

USEFUL
ADDRESSES AND
TELEPHONE NUMBERS

UK

Action Against Allergy
23/24 George Street
Richmond
Surrey TW9 1JY
Tel: 020 8892 2711
(A charity supplying information,
talks and books about allergies and
intolerances)

**Association for the Study of
   Obesity**
www.aso.org.uk

British Heart Foundation
14 Fitzhardinge Street
London W1H 6DH
Tel: 020 7935 0185
Fax: 020 7486 5820
Email: internet@bhf.org.uk
www.bhf.org.uk

British Nutrition Foundation
High Holborn House
52-54 High Holborn
London WC1V 6RQ
Tel: 020 7404 6504
Fax: 020 7404 6747
Email: postbox@nutrition.org.uk
www.nutrition.org.uk

Cancer Research UK
P.O. Box 123
Lincoln's Inn Fields
London WC2A 3PX
Tel: 020 7242 0200
Fax: 020 7269 3100
www.cancerresearchuk.org

Diabetes UK
10 Parkway
London NW1 7AA
Tel: 020 7424 1000
Fax: 020 7424 1001
Email: info@diabetes.org.uk
www.diabetes.org.uk

Food Standards Agency
Aviation House
125 Kingsway
London WC2B 6NH
Tel: 020 7276 8000
www.foodstandards.gov.uk

Institute of Food Research
Norwich Research Park
Colney
Norwich NR4 7UA
Tel: 01603 255000
Fax: 01603 507723
Email: ifr.communications@bbsrc.ac.uk
www.ifrn.bbsrc.ac.uk

INDEX

RECIPES

ACKNOWLEDGEMENTS

I would like to thank my clients who not only shared their recipes and snack ideas with me, but also inspired me to write this book. I would also like to thank my friend Dr. Julia Goedecke for checking the manuscript for technical correctness and sharing her knowledge with me. Thank you to Malinda, Dianne, Jessica and Michelle for all your help and support in the practices and especially to Dianne who contributed greatly to the section on children. Thanks to Linda, Joy and Beverley at Struik for all your efforts. And lastly to my loved ones, for your love, support and understanding.

KAREN PROTHEROE

First published in the UK in 2003 by
New Holland Publishers (UK) Ltd
Garfield House, 86–88 Edgware Road
London W2 2EA
United Kingdom
www.newhollandpublishers.com

First published in South Africa in 2002

1 3 5 7 9 10 8 6 4 2

Publishing Manager: Linda de Villiers
Editor: Joy Clack
Designer: Beverley Dodd
Illustrator: Sean Robertson
Indexer: Mary Lennox

Reproduction by Hirt & Carter Cape (Pty) Ltd
Printed and bound by Kyodo Printing, Singapore

ISBN 1 84330 514 3